Wakefield Press

Four Years in a Red Coat

Hiroko Cockerill is an honorary research fellow at the University of Queensland, specialising in translation studies. Her research includes books and articles about the translations of Futabatei Shimei. She has translated several books, from Russian to Japanese and from Japanese to English.

Peter Monteath is Professor of History at Flinders University in Adelaide. He has a particular interest in the history of internment and prisoners of war.

Dr Yuriko Nagata is an Honorary Senior Research Fellow with the School of Languages and Cultures of the University of Queensland. Her book *Unwanted Aliens* (1996, UQ press) is a standard reference work on Japanese internment in Australia during World War II.

Mr Koike in Japan in 1993

FOUR YEARS IN A RED COAT

THE LOVEDAY INTERNMENT CAMP DIARY OF MIYAKATSU KOIKE

TRANSLATED BY HIROKO COCKERILL

EDITED WITH AN INTRODUCTION BY
PETER MONTEATH AND YURIKO NAGATA

Wakefield
Press

Wakefield Press
16 Rose Street
Mile End
South Australia 5031
www.wakefieldpress.com.au

First published 2022

Cover designed by Stacey Zass
Typeset by Michael Deves, Wakefield Press

ISBN 978 1 74305 896 1

A catalogue record for this
book is available from the
National Library of Australia

Wakefield Press thanks
Coriole Vineyards for
continued support

Toshiba
International
Foundation

柳営日記

四年間の赤服生活

古池三八俵 著

CONTENTS

Acknowledgements

We wish to thank Mr Yasuo Koike, son of the author, Mr Miyakatsu Koike, for his generosity in making *Yokuryū Nikki* (1987) available for English translation, and for his help in providing photographs.

Mr Koike senior put together the notes and papers he kept from the war years and self-published them as a book in 1987. However, he did not register the book with an ISBN code. It took us many months to locate Mr Koike's family to obtain permission. Due to Covid-19 throughout 2020 and 2021 in Japan, the search was entirely entrusted to people in Japan. We sincerely thank the following who offered help in this search and list their names in alphabetical order:

Mr Doi, Shōji of Wakayama

Ms Koyama, Hatsumi, Kanagawa

Ms Miyake, Masako, Okayama

Mr Nagai, Yasuji, Asahi Newspaper, Osaka

Without the help from these people, this translation project would not have been possible.

Lastly, we thank the translator herself, Dr Hiroko Cockerill of Brisbane. Special thanks go also to Dr Alan Cockerill, who provided invaluable editorial and technical assistance.

We hope this publication will expand our understanding of the civilian internment experience in Australia during World War II through the words of a Japanese internee who spent four years behind the barbed wire at Loveday.

INTRODUCTION:
FOUR YEARS IN A RED COAT

Miyakatsu Koike lived the life of a diligent employee of the Yokohama Specie Bank in Surabaya in what was then the Dutch East Indies (DEI). He arrived there in 1935 and was joined by his wife, Fumiko, shortly after. Surabaya was one of the major pre-war Japanese commercial centres in DEI. They enjoyed life there among the expatriates' families. To Miyakatsu those years seemed like an eternal summer; outside of work he spent his days playing tennis or golf, pursuing his hobby of photography, and travelling.

On 8 December 1941 his entire world was turned on its head, because on that day he was arrested by the Dutch authorities. Fumiko had already been repatriated to Japan in July 1941. Dramatic events far away in Hawaii the previous day meant that for him, and millions like him, the world would never be the same again. Though he could have no inkling of it at the time, internment and a hellish voyage to a part of the world of which he had, at best, the vaguest understanding awaited him. In distant South Australia he would don the clothing that would both define and stigmatise him for the next four years of his life – a red coat.

Koike bore no personal responsibility for his plight. He had no say in the unleashing of the 'Greater East Asia War', and with it a bloody new phase in a conflict already raging on the other side of the world. As Japanese armies plotted the invasion of Malaya and the capture of Fortress Singapore, Koike and other Japanese living and working in DEI could not be untouched by the seismic events shaking the region. His arrest might have seemed an affront to natural justice, but, in the context of the time, it was also an inevitability.

After a month enduring the hardships of an internment camp called Sumowono in central Java, Koike and his fellow internees were taken to Batavia – today's Jakarta – and the port of Tanjung Priok. Here they commenced their journey to Adelaide's Outer Harbor in a tub called the *Cremer*. From there a train transported them, wide-eyed, as they crossed the parched plains separating Adelaide from the Murray, to their final destination, Loveday.

INTERNMENT IN AUSTRALIA

In both world wars internment in Australia is associated above all with the detention of 'enemy aliens'. That was the sinister-sounding name for those nationals of enemy states, who, for whatever reason, happened to find themselves in Australia after hostilities commenced. In the First World War that mainly meant Germans, whether they had been in Australia for days or decades. In time it even came to include some who had been 'naturalised' or were 'natural born' Australians.

In the Second World War, it was Germans again who were selectively targeted for internment from the moment Robert Menzies performed his 'melancholy duty' to announce that Australia was once again at war. Italians followed after Mussolini's entry into the war in June 1940, though the security authorities again confined their first visits to those who had already drawn attention to themselves. People of other nationalities would also find their way into the system of internment camps set up across the continent. Patterns of arrival and departure followed the fortunes of the war, as well as the ebb and flow of national anxieties at home.

Japan's entry brought the war to the Pacific theatre, which threatened Australia's national security more directly. The internment of Japanese was well-anticipated, and almost all the members of the Japanese migrant community in Australia were rounded up within the day of Japan's bombing of Pearl Harbor on 7 December 1941. Under the White Australia Policy the Japanese community was always much smaller than that of Germans and Italians. In July 1941, 1,171 Japanese over 16 years old were registered as aliens. There was a heavy concentration in the north, where they were engaged in the pearl-shell industry. Australia rounded up 1,141 Japanese, who accounted for 97% of the registered Japanese, while only 31% of Italians and 32% of Germans were interned.[1]

However, many of the internees detained in Australia were brought here from other parts of the world. In the First World War German nationals – mainly men, but women and children too – were brought to Australia from such places as Singapore, Hong Kong, New Guinea and Sri Lanka. In the Second World War they came from British-controlled parts of the world even further afield: Palestine and Iran, the Straits Settlements, and even Britain itself.

Ultimately, in the Second World War the number of civilian internees from other parts of the world came to outnumber those who had been in Australia when the war began. They were brought to Australia not only to lighten Britain's load of 'enemy aliens', but also to ease the burden on Australia's Free French and Dutch allies. Altogether some 8,000 were transported to Australia for internment, outnumbering the roughly 7,000 already here.[2] Thirty nationalities were represented among those numbers.

Of those sent to Australia, 3,160 were Japanese. They comprised 1,949 from DEI, 1,124 from New Caledonia, 50 from New Zealand, 34

---

1 Y. Nagata, *Unwanted Aliens: Japanese Internment in Australia*, Brisbane: University of Queensland Press, 1996, p. 60.

2 National Archives of Australia, 'Wartime internment camps in Australia', https://www.naa.gov.au/explore-collection/immigration-and-citizenship/wartime-internment-camps-australia (accessed 28 February 2021).

from the New Hebrides and 3 from the Solomon Islands.[3] Among these, approximately 600 Formosans (Taiwanese) and some Koreans were included in those from DEI. They were arrested as Japanese, because Formosa and Korea were then under Japanese control.

The Australian military authorities ran Australia's network of POW camps as well as its internment camps, so that a visitor to both kinds of camp might have been hard-pressed at first to notice the difference. The layout of these camps, the barbed wire, the buildings, and even the guards themselves, were virtually identical. Indeed, in some cases camps served to detain civilians and POWs, though not at the same time.

There was one other factor that helps to explain the similarities between the camps, and that is in the realm of international law. Australia had become a signatory of the 1929 'Geneva Convention Relative to the Treatment of Prisoners of War' and was legally bound to uphold its obligations under that Convention. Efforts had been made to adopt a similar Convention relative to the treatment of civilian internees, but with those efforts still in train when war broke out, states generally agreed to apply the terms for POWs to civilians also. Australia was one of those states.

There were, however, some crucial differences as well. While all POWs in Australia were men, the population of civilian internees included women and children, albeit in smaller numbers. Family groups and women were held in camps in Tatura, Victoria, while male internees over 16 years of age were sent to Loveday in South Australia or Hay in NSW.[4] If Koike's wife, Fumiko, had not been repatriated to Japan before

---

3 [Prisoners of War (Australia) and Internees – General:] History – Report on Directorate of Prisoners of War and Internees at Army Headquarters Melbourne 1939–1951. AWM54, 780/1/6, Part 1, p. 93.

4 Unattached males over 16 years old were held at Loveday and Hay, but in April 1943 a major reorganisation of internees took place due to a change of the UK policy to reclassify internees who were merchant seamen as POWs. Approximately 500 Japanese were previously engaged in the pearling industry in Australia and were reclassified from internees to PWJMs (that is, Japanese Prisoners of War). They were concentrated at Hay, while the other males remained at Loveday.

the outbreak of the war, they would have been sent together to Tatura.

According to the Geneva Convention, military officers and NCOs could not be required to work, but Other Ranks among the POW population could. Civilian internees, on the other hand, could not be forced to work, though they could be given the option. Koike, as we read in his diary, was one of the many internees who elected to work. Internees engaged in tasks as various as cutting wood at one of the work camps attached to Loveday, helping at the piggery, or harvesting poppies for morphine. While inside their compounds, the internees could wear civilian clothing, but when they were outside – typically on labour duties – the strictly enforced rule was that they were to wear army-issue clothing dyed a burgundy colour. It was to identify them as internees and render escape difficult. For Koike, the red clothing he wore became such a part of his identity that he chose it for the title of his diary recording his years of internment.

The Australian authorities had few reservations in inviting Japanese civilian internees to take on such work. They had a reputation for being docile and compliant. On the other hand, the Japanese POWs accommodated famously at the POW camp in Cowra were not required to work, though the Other Ranks among them could have been. The Australians were well aware of the radically different attitude the Japanese POWs brought to their detention. For many of them, their very capture had been a source of great shame. The injunction issued to them had been to sacrifice their life for the Emperor rather than surrender. They typically sought to conceal the truth of their capture by providing false names and electing not to communicate with their families in Japan, lest their ignominy be spread at home as well. Where opportunities to escape presented themselves, as they did on the night of 5 August 1944 in Cowra, then the Japanese POWs would not forego the chance to put their shame behind them, even if it meant death. 234 men died as a result of the mass breakout. The civilian internees were very different.

LOVEDAY INTERNMENT CAMPS

Loveday, gazetted as a town in February 1940, is located just outside the Riverland township of Barmera.[5] It lent itself to use as an internment camp site for a number of reasons. Located far from the coast, there seemed little risk that any escapees would be able to flee the country. At the same time, good road and railway connections meant that it would be possible to deliver large numbers of internees – and their guards – to Loveday. Electricity and telephone communications, too, were readily at hand, along with local services such as a hospital.[6] Irrigation systems drawing on the nearby Murray River meant that the surrounding land could be cultivated, and indeed in time Loveday would become a rich source of a variety or crops and other primary produce.

The first two camps at Loveday, known as Camp 9 and Camp 10 and comprising in both cases a Camp HQ and rectangular-shaped compound designed for 1,000 persons, were built about 2 kilometres apart by civilian contractors. Though instructions for the building of a facility were issued as early as July 1940, Loveday did not receive the first of its internees until 11 June 1941.[7] On that day, 458 Italians arrived from Hay in New South Wales. On the following day, a further 502 arrived, including the captain and crew of the Italian vessel *Romolo*, sunk by HMAS *Manoora* near Cape York days after Italy entered the war.[8] Along with Italians, Camp 10 came also to house Germans, brought to Australia through an agreement with the British government.

Camp 14 was built after Japan entered the war, and with the realisation

---

5   A. Lyell McEwan, 'Town of Loveday', *The South Australian Government Gazette*, 1 February 1940, p. 170. http://www8.austlii.edu.au/au/other/sa_gazette/1940/5/170. pdf (accessed 28 February 2021).

6   Peter Monteath, *Captured Lives: Australia's Wartime Internment Camps*, Canberra: NLA Publishing, 2018, p. 147.

7   Committee appointed to record the History of Internment in South Australia, *History of Loveday: Loveday Internment Group*, Barmera, 1940–1946. Adelaide: Committee appointed to record the History of Internment in South Australia, 1946, p. 5.

8   *History of Loveday*, p 5.

that agreements struck with the Dutch East Indies and Free French authorities would mean that Australia could soon expect a new wave of internees from overseas. It was of quite a different design than the first two, comprising as it did four compounds inside one perimeter, with roads running north-south and east-west to separate the compounds. Inside each compound were the facilities with which Miyakatsu Koike would become intimately familiar. There were eighteen sleeping huts, four mess halls, two large kitchens, two latrines, two wash-houses and ablution blocks, as well as work and hobby huts. In addition, one of the compounds, 14B, contained a hospital block. Japanese internees were held in compounds 14B and 14C. 14A held Italians and later Germans. Generally speaking, the authorities sought to accommodate different nationalities in separate compounds, but this was not always possible. In particular, many different nationalities were gathered together in 14D, which had members of as many as 28 nationalities detained in it, both local and overseas.[9]

The first Japanese internees, 49 of them, were escorted into 14B on 5 January 1942. They had been arrested in Darwin and brought down from a temporary camp at Adelaide River in the Northern Territory.[10] They were soon joined by Japanese from New Caledonia. On 30 January the first batch of Japanese from DEI arrived. They were taken into the neighbouring compound, 14C, under the command of Major Andrew Lott.[11] By March, that compound was just 30 short of its nominal maximum capacity of 1,000.[12]

During the first twelve months, transfers and reorganisations of internees took place between compounds and camps. On 15 August 1942, a major reduction took place as a result of 528 Japanese being released from Loveday to be included in the first prisoner exchange between Japan

---

9 *Ibid.*, p. 14.
10 *Ibid.*, p. 6.
11 *Ibid.*
12 *Ibid.*

and the United Kingdom and Dominion governments.[13] The Japanese Government nominated individuals, but there were a lot of mistakes and confusion with the romanisation of Japanese names.[14] The 528 were part of the total of 871 internees, including 343 from the Hay and Tatura camps. They embarked on the exchange ship the *City of Canterbury* in Melbourne on 18 August 1942. After this reduction in numbers at Loveday, Koike and his fellow DEI internees were moved to 14B. Not all of them were there for long, however, as Koike's diary tells us. He himself was mysteriously absent from the vital lists of those 528 Japanese internees released from Loveday. Those who remained would live in the hope that the second repatriation might be offered them, too, but they were disappointed. There would be no early release for them, and indeed even after the end of the war their patience would be tested further.

In general, they seem to have adjusted to their fate with stoic calm. Their captors later summed up the Japanese internees as follows: 'Subservient, were model prisoners. Their fanatical desire to maintain "face" made them easy to handle in their eagerness to obey all orders and instructions to the letter.'[15]

In May 1943, the Loveday Group held a combined number of 5,382 internees.[16] The maximum population at any time during the course of the war would have been around that mark, although in the last couple of years of the war the population declined. The security fears that had provoked waves of internments subsided, and economic priorities demanded that the camp system not be an unnecessarily large burden on the government. In February 1944 Camps 9 and 10 were vacated, leaving all who remained in the four compounds of Camp 14. When half of them were emptied in January 1945, it was only the Japanese who remained.[17]

---

13 *Ibid.*
14 Nagata, *Unwanted Aliens*, p. 97.
15 *History of Loveday*, p. 10.
16 *Ibid.*, p. 7.
17 *Ibid.*, p. 8.

Not surprisingly then, when VE-Day was announced in Loveday, the authorities noted that the nearly 2,000 Japanese 'were amazed, but not outwardly interested'.[18] In contrast, the authorities clearly approached the proclamation of VP-Day with some trepidation, issuing firm instructions to the Japanese compound leaders that there was to be no factional fighting and that everyone was to carry out the work set them. True to their generally acquiescent behaviour throughout their internment, the Japanese carried out the instructions in their entirety. At the same time, camp officers reported that a large percentage of the internees did not believe that Japan had been defeated.[19] This was the same with other Japanese held at Tatura and Hay.

Memories of Loveday vary widely. The camp's official history paints an altogether rosy picture of an institution that was an 'unqualified success',[20] not only meeting the obligation to hold large numbers of internees securely but also benefitting the wider community – and indeed the war effort – through its successful conversion to a site of agricultural production.

Against that, there are those who insist on the essential injustice of prolonged detention without trial, even in times of war. While there may well have been genuine security risks, many of Loveday's detainees were not merely harmless, but regarded themselves as loyal Australians. Their capture and detention was an affront to them, an unjustifiable burden on their families, a blight on their communities, and an indelible stain on Australia's war record. While conditions might have been materially adequate, the cost on the longer term mental and physical health of internees, and in the burden of resentment, is inestimable. The costs of internment were carried disproportionately by Japanese internees, many of them elderly from the moment of their arrest, and of those a significant number perished in captivity, a long way from family and friends.

---

18 *Ibid.*
19 *Ibid.*
20 *Ibid.*, p. 21.

By far the highest mortality rate among the 135 dead at Loveday was that of the Japanese: 108 of them died there.[21] Readers of Koike's diary will note the all-too-frequent accounts of the passing of his countrymen. At first they were buried in the Barmera War Cemetery, but, in 1964, their remains were transferred to Cowra, where the Japanese government created a Japanese Cemetery with the help of the Australian government. They were interred with the remains of Japanese POWs who died at the mass breakout.

CONCLUSION

The Australian government released internees of European origin as soon as fighting stopped and some even before the end of the war. Internees from Britain or Europe generally could stay in Australia. They joined the rest of the population for the post-war reconstruction of Australia. However, the Australian government was firm with the treatment of the Japanese. Only a small number of local Japanese were granted release before the cessation of hostilities with Japan.[22] After the war, the Australian Government granted just over 100 Japanese continuing residency. They were Australian-born themselves or had Australian-born members in their family. The overseas Japanese were outside Australia's responsibility and were destined to be sent to Japan.

Not until 20 February 1946, almost 6 months after Japan's surrender, did Loveday's Japanese farewell their home of four years. On that day three special trains departed the Barmera Railway Station for Port Melbourne, with 1,650 Japanese men on board. The next day they embarked on the *Kōei maru* for Japan where they were joined by Japanese women and family groups from Tatura and also 400 Japanese POWs from Murchison POW camp near Tatura, nearly 3,000 in all. The second repatriation ship, the *Daikaku maru*, carried the Japanese men from Hay, including 2,691 POWs,

---

21 *Ibid.*, p. 25.
22 Nagata, *Unwanted Aliens*, p. 120.

and 500 Japanese merchant seamen (PWJM). They left Sydney on 2 March 1946.[23] The departure of Loveday's Japanese took place on the last day of February, bringing wartime civilian interment in South Australia to its conclusion.[24] This time it was a convoy of motor vehicles that departed Loveday, bearing Formosans (Taiwanese) to Sydney. It was a Japanese destroyer, formally named the *Yoizuki*, but for good reasons sometimes known as the 'hell ship'. The *Yoizuki* sailed on 6 March carrying 1,005 Formosan and Korean internees and POWs.[25]

Miyakatsu Koike was among those on the *Kōei maru* when it cast off from Port Melbourne at 6.45 on the evening of 21 February. The *Kōei maru* arrived at Uraga in Japan on 13 March. Koike returned home to a Japan devastated by war and played his part in returning it to prosperity. He learned about the deaths of members of his family during the war, including his father and his own first child. He continued to work at the Tokyo Bank (formerly the Yokohama Specie Bank) until his retirement in 1959. Nonetheless, he never forgot his four years in a red coat. He started to compile the notes he brought back from Loveday into a book and published it in 1987, then distributed copies to his colleagues' families. Mr Koike died from a heart attack on 22 December 1998, at the age of 93. His wife, Fumiko, suddenly passed away during his funeral. They are both buried in Koike's birthplace in Konan, Aichi.

---

23 Nagata, *Unwanted Aliens*, p. 200.
24 *History of Loveday*, p. 9.
25 *Ibid.*, p. 18.

A NOTE ON THE TEXT

When he finally published his diary recording his years of internment in distant Loveday in South Australia, Miyakatsu Koike advised his readers, 'I humbly present this book as a maiden work by an amateur writer'. A handwritten note added, 'I should acknowledge that there is some ambiguity in my memory of the internment camp in Australia'. By profession Miyakatsu Koike was, after all, an employee of a bank. When a limited edition of his recollections became available in 1987, primarily for the benefit of his friends and former employees of the Tokyo Bank (formerly the Yokohama Specie Bank), he had been back in Japan for over four decades, and he was 82 years of age. No wonder that he cautioned his readers about the reliability of his memories.

Nonetheless, *Four Years in a Red Coat* is an invaluable record of one man's experience of war in Australia. While his memories might have faded, Koike's diary faithfully records the everyday challenges faced by him and thousands like him. For civilian internees, the lived experience of war was not primarily about cataclysmic moments of life-shattering violence. Rather, war was about the stoic conquest of smaller, daily challenges, the calm observance of routine, the endurance of discomfort and privation, and the hope that at some unknown time their former lives would be restored to them.

That Koike chose to publish his diary as an octogenarian is a sign that his feat of quiet endurance shaped the rest of his life. It continued to connect him to others in a kind of community of shared experiences. Happily, he chose to include next to his words the images made by others as a way, not just of recording, but of dealing with lives of constraint. Those images are reproduced in this translation also, alongside some of the Australian images of life in Loveday.

Peter Monteath and Yuriko Nagata

PREFACE

I received instructions to transfer to the Surabaya branch of the Yokohama Specie Bank (located in Java, Indonesia) in May 1935, and at the end of May I left Kobe on the *Suwa maru*, which was owned by Nippon Yūsen [the NKY Line]. The ship called in at Shanghai and Hong Kong, and then in Singapore I changed from the *Suwa maru* to a ship owned by KPM.[1] After a three-week voyage, I finally arrived in Surabaya. From that time, I spent a little over six years in that land of perpetual summer. When I look back over my entire life, it seems to me that I lived a full life during that period. I was able to enjoy my spare time to the full, playing tennis or golf, taking photos, and travelling.

However, when the Greater East Asia War [the Pacific War] broke out on 8 December 1941, my life suddenly changed, and I was arrested by the Dutch East Indies. After being detained for a month, I was transported under guard to Adelaide, South Australia, on the *Cremer*, which was referred to as a hell ship. That was at the end of January 1942. Then I was compelled to spend a dreary life in a red coat for about four years in the Loveday Internment Camp, which was built in a remote area near the desert, in a vast expanse of bleak plains on the Australian continent. We all waited impatiently for the day of our release and encouraged each other to survive until we could set foot on the soil of our motherland.

---

1 Koninklijke Paketvaart-Maatschappij, or simply KPM, was a Dutch shipping company operating in the Dutch East Indies, now Indonesia.

In August 1942, an exchange of internees was carried out between Japan and England. Unfortunately, I was not in the repatriation group, due to some error by the Red Cross. However, in March 1946 I arrived safely in Uraga on a repatriation ship. I was thankful to be home at last. Although I am inexperienced as a writer, I shall attempt to write an internment camp diary, relying on scant records and on my memory. I hope that it will help children to understand the misery caused by the war and the importance of peace.

Now that more than forty years have passed since the end of the Second World War, I can look back on life in the internment camp with some nostalgia. The faces of more than seven hundred people, with whom I spent time in the camp, emerge vividly before me. Unfortunately, I have had no contact with most of them. Presumably, some have already departed this world. However, if I get the chance to meet any who are still alive, I would like to talk to them and reflect on our past together.

Finally, to all the people who sadly died in the remote land of southern Australia, I would like to tell you that our motherland recovered quickly from defeat and became the second strongest economic power in the world. Please watch over the progress of our motherland and rest in peace.

November 1987

At the age of 82, the Author

CHAPTER 1

BEFORE DETENTION

The second round of economic negotiations between Japan and the Dutch East Indies was suspended following the withdrawal of the Ambassador Extraordinary and Plenipotentiary Mr Yoshizawa at the end of June 1941.[1] Nevertheless, at that time the leaders of the two countries issued a joint statement that they would maintain friendly relations as in the past. From that time, the trade relationship between the two countries continued, albeit somewhat erratically. Through a sort of clearing arrangement concluded between the Yokohama Specie Bank and the Java Bank, import-export trade was secured to a certain extent. However, due to tight exchange controls maintained by the Dutch East Indies government, the goods that could be traded were inevitably restricted, and munitions that our country wished to import were barred. Consequently, Japan developed a large export surplus in the balance of trade.

Once our army advanced into southern French Indochina, the Dutch East Indies government followed the United States of America, and on 28 July all assets of Japanese people were frozen on the territory of the Dutch East Indies. Under these circumstances, all Japanese people tried to bear the unbearable, and we made a huge effort to continue our business. We were compelled to open but transacted no business at all. In the end,

---

1 Kenkichi Yoshizawa, a former foreign minister of Japan, was sent as a special envoy to the Dutch East Indies to present a set of strict demands to the government in Batavia; he withdrew without agreement.

the continued existence of our businesses was threatened. Each trading company tried to wind down its operations and at the same time hastened to conclude any unfinished business in preparation for withdrawal. At this time, the Japanese consulate also made secret preparations for the repatriation of ordinary Japanese people. It appeared that the consulate was attempting to avoid the worst situation, and many Japanese people residing there disposed of their property and gathered in Surabaya, where a ship would sail for Japan. Although many Japanese people gathered there, they spent day after day doing nothing, while they waited for the ship.

At that time, the amount of money people could bring back to Japan was limited to five hundred guilders (equivalent to one thousand one hundred and eleven yen). After pondering over this situation, many people decided to buy a diamond ring or an expensive watch. There were other people who changed all their guilders into yen to take their money to Japan. Unfortunately, many of them had their yen confiscated by a customs officer when they went on board. At that time, it was prohibited to bring hundred-yen notes circulating in the occupied territory in China home to Japan. Consequently, most hundred-yen notes flew to the Dutch East Indies. As a result, people could obtain yen at less than half the official rate. (For example, to transfer a hundred yen through a bank, you had to pay forty-five guilders. At the same time, you could buy a hundred yen for twenty guilders.) However, as the government of the Dutch East Indies strictly prohibited people from taking out Japanese yen notes, it was impossible to transfer Japanese yen notes by any official route. Consequently, people who bought Japanese yen notes tried either to sew them into their clothes, or to make a double-bottomed coffee tin and conceal them in that, or to conceal them in a soap box. It appeared that these various means of smuggling yen failed, as most of them were discovered at customs. These failed attempts were revealed when the confiscated goods were sent to the Japanese consulate after the last repatriation ship, the *Fuji maru*, sailed for Japan. We heard that a large number of yen notes were discovered. Apart from the above-mentioned methods, people even concealed hundred-yen notes in the soles of shoes, or skilfully hid them in a suitcase. The most miserable case I heard was of a person who lived in Semarang, who disposed of all his property and changed all his money into yen to take to Japan. Unfortunately, a customs officer discovered all his Japanese yen notes, and confiscated them.

As far as the Surabaya branch of the Yokohama Specie Bank was concerned, the manager at that time, Mr Kaizō Sakimura, was anxious about our immediate future, as economic negotiations between Japan and the Dutch East Indies had been suspended. He made the following decisions:

(a) All families of bank staff, and some of the bank staff themselves, should be repatriated. Firstly, in May 1941, cabins were booked for the families. The first family group embarked on their homeward voyage on the *Kitano maru* from Surabaya on 16 July. For the second group, consisting of only the family of the manager, a cabin was booked on the *Haruna maru*, which was scheduled to leave at the end of July. However, when the order to freeze assets was issued on 28 July, the *Haruna maru* suddenly disappeared. We were crestfallen, but fortunately the ship arrived in Batavia at the end of the month and the family returned home safely.

The repatriation of the family groups went so smoothly that some Japanese people became jealous and wondered whether the Yokohama Specie Bank had gathered some special information beforehand. However, as the families of the Yokohama Specie Bank's Batavia branch and the staff and families of the Mitsui and Mitsubishi companies also boarded the *Haruna maru*, it is unlikely that Mr Sakimura was the only one to receive special information. I would rather give credit to Mr Sakimura for his keen insight into the situation, as his decision to repatriate the staff and their family was the correct one, however unfortunate it may have been.

As far as the bank staff were concerned, his decision was as follows. Many trading companies' employees were still staying at hotels without doing anything after the order to freeze assets was issued. The Yokohama Specie Bank began repatriating staff ahead of these trading companies. The number of bank staff remaining behind was to be kept to only two or three, and the rest were to be repatriated one after another. We were waiting for a favourable opportunity, but the visit of a Japanese ship had not yet been scheduled. In the end, staff were repatriated by a ship of the Java-China Line via Manila and Shanghai.

(b) With customers, we tried to minimise the scale of our business and recommended that they repatriate as soon as they finished winding up their affairs. As a result, there were only a few full-time staff left in most trading companies after the *Fuji maru* sailed to Japan. Under these circumstances, our bank was open, but transacting no business. We thus dealt solely with money carried by people who were returning to Japan. (I shall not go into detail about the work undertaken by the bank to prepare for repatriation.)

After the *Haruna maru* left Java at the end of July, no Japanese repatriation ship arrived for some time. Finally, the *Takachiho maru* arrived in the middle of October, and then the *Fuji maru* arrived in November. In this way, almost all Japanese people living in the eastern part of Java were repatriated to their motherland. Our bank had only two staff left, apart from the general manager and the deputy general manager. We worked intensely to wind up any unsettled business, anticipating that we should all board the next repatriation ship. In December we received an order from the head office to close the branch. Branch business was scheduled to continue until 10 December and then the branch would be closed. As soon as we finished winding up any outstanding business, we would assemble at the Batavia branch. We were focused on preparing the documents that we would take back to Japan.

On 6 December we received instructions to make an advanced settlement of accounts on 8 December. Consequently, although it was a Sunday, we went to our office on 7 December. We raced against the clock to prepare the settlement of our accounts. On the way home, I dropped into the Surabaya branch of the Mitsubishi Bank, which was next to us. I found that the branch manager, Mr Aiji Sakurai, and the deputy branch manager, Masaji Kunieda, were also absorbed in preparing documents to take back to Japan. Mr Sakurai told me that the repatriation ship that we were expecting might not come due to the tense situation. There was a fifty-fifty chance that the ship would come.

New Year's gathering with colleagues' families in Surabaya, 1941. Mr Koike is in the middle of the back row; his wife Fumiko is seated second from left.
Courtesy Yasuo Koike

Miyakatsu Koike in Surabaya before the war, date unknown.
Courtesy Yasuo Koike.

In Surabaya, year unknown. Miyakatsu Koike is on the far left, Fumiko on the far right. Courtesy Yasuo Koike.

Group photo of a gathering of the Surabaya Friendship Association in 1987.

After the war, at the office of Tokyo Bank (previously Yokohama Specie Bank).
Mr Koike is seated in the centre. Courtesy Yasuo Koike.

Mr Koike is fourth from the left in the third row from the front. Courtesy Yasuo Koike.

Mr Koike with his wife Fumiko and grandchildren in 1987 in Japan.
Courtesy Yasuo Koike.

Mr Koike with his wife, Fumiko, in 1993 in Japan.
Courtesy Yasuo Koike.

CHAPTER 2

MEMOIR OF DETENTION BY THE DUTCH EAST INDIES AUTHORITIES

8 December 1941 was the day for the advanced settlement of accounts ahead of the closing of the branch two days later. (When I reflect on those days, the instructions from the head office may have been intended as a warning.) By seven o'clock in the morning I and two other lodgers had already finished breakfast, and we made ourselves comfortable for a while before going to the office. Taking the opportunity, I went to check the residence of the manager Mr Sakimura, who was away. When I finished checking the residence and drove my car to its entrance, I suddenly noticed that more than ten police officers were bustling around in front of the entrance to return to my communal residence. The police officers were understandably confused, as nobody opened the door. The manager's residence, which had been still and calm only minutes earlier, was suddenly besieged by armed police.

My instinct had told me that this day would come, and I was prepared for it. As the police had given no explanation, I could easily imagine that they had come to arrest any Japanese people. Nevertheless, I could not understand why two trucks full of policemen were required. I got out of my car to seek some explanation and greeted the Dutch East Indies policeman who seemed to be in charge. He told me that they had come to arrest the manager. I replied that the manager had gone to Batavia on a business trip. He then asked me to accompany him to search the manager's residence.

Because the manager lived on his own and furnishings were limited, the search did not last long. The two policemen who accompanied us held a gun to my back all the time. After they confirmed that the manager was away, I went back to my car intending to return home to my communal residence, but the officer in charge ordered two local policemen into my car to take me to the police station. I insisted that I was not the person to be arrested and that I was not properly dressed, as I was not yet going to my office. I was not wearing proper shoes, nor a proper jacket. Citing the example that when a German person was arrested, he was allowed to take a suitcase full of personal belongings, I insisted that I needed to go home to my communal residence. However, my request was rejected, and they took me to the police station in place of my manager.

The car passed in front of the communal residence where I had lived for so long. The gate was tightly shut and guarded by several armed policemen. It seemed calm and quiet. I sighed. Today the bank car was functioning differently to the day before ... Today it was carrying bank staff as prisoners to the police station ... As soon as the car arrived at the police headquarters, I was taken to the chief of police and was asked the name of the hotel where the manager was staying. I replied that he was staying in the Hotel des Indes, and he immediately telephoned to Batavia. The chief of police was agitated and told me, 'This morning Japan has declared war upon Britain and the United States, and consequently the Dutch East Indies government has declared war upon Japan. We are consequently detaining all Japanese people.' He ordered for me to be taken to another room. I asked if I could go back to the communal residence to fetch my jacket and shoes. He then arranged for my chauffeur to go there to fetch them.

Thanks to this arrangement, I regained possession of my jacket and shoes, but I was not able to get my emergency suitcase (in which I had placed toilet articles, underwear, and medicine).

When I was taken to the other room, I was greeted by Mr Asao Togami (the deputy manager of the Surabaya branch of the Yokohama Specie Bank,) and Mr Shōichi Fujii (an employee of the Surabaya branch of the Yokohama Specie Bank). Neither of my colleagues had been able to take anything with them apart from the work clothes they were wearing. Thus, pitifully, we all found ourselves to have nothing but the clothes we wore. Nevertheless, we congratulated each other on our honourable detention for our motherland and vowed that we would behave prudently from now on.

I felt that the clock was ticking extremely slowly. I meditated for several minutes sitting on my chair, and gradually regained my calm. I was pondering over the incidents that had happened that morning, when the weather suddenly changed. It had been fine in the morning, but the sky suddenly changed colour. Rain drops started falling from the sky. I turned my eyes to the entrance of the police headquarters, and saw that Japanese people were being taken into custody one after another in cars or in the sidecars of motorcycles. I also noticed that trucks full of policemen frequently passed by on the road in front of the police headquarters. The sea of steel helmets and the noise of canons being pulled by tractors ... everything reminded me of the outbreak of war. Everything vividly reminded me of the tense situation of our motherland, tears involuntarily welled up in my eyes, and my head spontaneously drooped.

We were surrounded by a group of local police officers armed with guns. We could not suppress a wry smile at this ostentatious guard. While the spooky silence continued, detained people were taken into the police headquarters one after another. Amongst the detained, there were some taken from the hospital. They were taken from their beds. It seemed the police judged that it was impossible to detain some of them, who were taken back to the hospital. Then it was decided that we three, a

Japanese person from mainland Japan,[1] and a medical doctor of Taiwanese nationality with two other family members, were to be taken to another place. We were separated and set out in three cars. Our cars advanced northwards through the familiar town, but our destination was completely unknown. Using our imaginations, we engaged in animated conversation about our destination, without paying any attention to the policeman in the car. From the car window we saw local people pointing at us and shouting, 'Look! The police are transporting Japanese!' After a while, we finally arrived at the town hall. It was around at 11 o'clock in the morning.

At the entrance of the town hall, which was being used as a temporary detention centre, a policeman who was known to me was standing. He told me, 'Please don't behave in a friendly manner today. I shall conduct a physical examination and search your personal belongings, as my duty dictates.' He quickly conducted a simple search and I took my chair to an appointed place and sat down. The people who were already seated there were Japanese people from mainland Japan, Taiwanese people, local people considered to be Japanese sympathisers or who were Japanologists, and Chinese people. They were about eighty in total. My paging number was 83. Amongst these people there were women holding children in their arms. Everyone sat properly on their chairs. We only exchanged nods and quietly waited for our orders. Meanwhile, detained people were brought into the town hall by the police one after another.

There were no signs of lunch preparations, even after noon. I suddenly felt tired, as I had been tense all morning. The time seemed to pass extremely slowly that day. As I had nothing else to do, I recalled the various incidents that had occurred … Although I was expecting this to happen, I was still badly shaken. I was also thinking of the situation at my bank office and wondering about its employees. Dark thoughts began to press

---

1 The Japanese word used here is 'naichi-jin', where 'naichi' refers to Japan proper, as opposed to the territories occupied in the period leading up to the Second World War, which were referred to as 'gaichi'.

in on me ... While I was lost in meditation, I went to sleep leaning on the chair. When I came to, I heard people talking to each other.

I did not feel very hungry, and to overcome my ennui I began talking to the people sitting next to me about our situation as detainees. Most people detained were taken from their homes, but some of them were taken from the company where they worked. Some people were even taken on their way to work. The funniest case was a person who was taken from a barbershop when his hair was only half cut. There were a few who wore sandals and a summer kimono. Two or three people were lucky enough to bring a suitcase with them. We received radio news about 'our navy attack on Pearl Harbor' from a Chinese person who was also detained. All felt revived by this good news and became cheerful again. Several groups spontaneously formed here and there, and people merrily discussed the actions of the Imperial Army. One person talked like an authority on military affairs and started suggesting future military operations for Japan to engage in. Listening to him, I again greatly appreciated the hardship experienced by the bravest Japanese soldiers at the front and sincerely hoped for their long-lasting good fortune in battle.

Around the town hall was strictly fenced off with barbed wire, and policemen were allocated at four- or five-meters intervals. What struck me as strange was that all the policemen on guard held a sword in their right hand and a gun in their left hand. In addition, a policeman with a drawn sword was standing near the toilet (only one toilet was allocated), and under his guard we were allowed to use the toilet one at a time. Consequently, a long queue formed to wait in turn. At around three o'clock in the afternoon the policemen were replaced by soldiers. We also noticed that a machine gun was set up at the entrance of the town hall. Soon after that, one tin of military ration food (flavoured rice) was distributed per person. We knew that we could not hope for drinking water, but we were disappointed that we were given neither chopsticks nor a spoon to eat with. We had no choice but to eat with a folded business card. We could not eat all the tinned rice with a folded business card and had to discard most of it. Up to then we had never experienced any inconvenience with food. What a big difference one day made! I deeply missed having a piece of bread, something I had not valued highly before. I also missed cool water or some fruit in the refrigerator. However, when I thought of our soldiers on the battlefield, I knew I should not complain. I again vowed to myself that I would endure everything and would never give up until the last minute, even if I were detained by an enemy country.

Arrests continued till the evening. One after another, people were arrested and taken to the town hall. There were no Japanese from mainland Japan, and most of them were Taiwanese and Chinese people. Amongst them I noted an innocent primary school child holding a school bag who had been taken directly from school. The long day finally ended, and at dusk I saw that all the staff members of the consulate except for Mr He, who was a Taiwanese national, were being transferred to a different location. Perhaps they were confined in the consulate.

Later, we were finally given a straw mat each and the chairs were taken away. Nobody guessed that this straw mat would be used as a bed for the night. At around eight o'clock in the evening the same military ration was again distributed to each of us, and everyone tried to eat quietly without any drinking water. Once again, we could not eat everything, and most of the food was wasted. At first sight, our dinner may have appeared reminiscent of a picnic scene under a sunny blue sky, with people merrily talking to each other and fully enjoying the sunshine. However, our straw mats were laid on a concrete floor, and we had to eat tasteless food in dim light. We felt sorry for ourselves. On the other hand, among the Chinese and Taiwanese people, there were some who had dinner merrily with food brought by their relatives. We could not expect such good fortune. When we lay down on our straw mats, we had neither a blanket nor a mosquito net. I took off my jacket and covered the upper part of my body with it, to protect myself from the army of mosquitoes and the cold morning air. I used my shoe as a pillow, but it was hard to go to sleep. However, I did imperceptibly fall sleep, due to exhaustion. When I regained consciousness, I could hear people's voices all around. Perhaps they too found it difficult to go to sleep and decided to talk all night. When I shut my eyes, memories of my arrest kept flashing before my mind's eye in rapid succession. I thought about the bank, the communal residence, and the fate of our employees over and over again, and it became even harder to fall asleep. It grew late, and fewer voices were heard. I became sleepy and fell asleep without knowing when. Perhaps it was one o'clock at night.

Just before dawn, I was woken by the cold air. Around the town hall a blackout was in force. In front of the hall army trucks came and went frequently. The night gave us no rest. At around four in the morning, people began getting up one after another and started talking over various things. We too got up, rubbing our eyes and waited for the dawn. Fatigue was clearly shown in each person's face. After a while, a violent soldier kicked a Chinese person's pillow and shouted at him, 'Wake up!' Then everyone got up all at once.

We looked at the violent soldier with reproach in our eyes and could not help feeling antagonism towards him. However, we were captives, and we tried hard to be prudent.

That was how we greeted the dawn of the second day of our captivity on 9 December.

On 9 December, an official told us that we were to be transferred to a different location. As the departure time was quickly approaching, we were not allowed to return home to fetch our personal belongings, though the president of the Japan Club had requested that we be allowed to do so the day before. It had thus finally been decided that we were to have nothing but the clothes which we wore. As a matter of fact, the night before we had been talking about the things that we would love to fetch if we were allowed to go back to our communal residence, such as tinned rice cake for the new year, various other kinds of tinned food, and clothes. All our talk was in vain. That morning we were given neither water to wash our face, nor breakfast. On top of that, the toilet was congested, and I had to wait more than thirty minutes for my turn.

Soon they made us form five lines in the front yard of the town hall. It was six o'clock in the morning. Our group consisted of Japanese people from mainland Japan and people of Taiwanese nationality. There were one hundred and forty of us in total (Chinese people were excluded). First, the commander in charge of transportation strictly checked the number of people to be transferred. Then he allocated soldiers to escort us. The soldiers loaded their guns with live bullets in front of us.

The town hall was surrounded by many curious city residents, and they watched us being transferred. At the departure signal we began marching quietly past these people. In front and behind us machine guns were positioned, and we were under strict guard. We looked like sheep being taken to an abattoir.

At half-past six in the morning we arrived at the yard of the Pasar Turi Station from which our train was to depart for Semarang. The train yard was under heavy guard. We passed through the soldiers' bristling bayonets. Then we were divided up to board three poorly lit third-class carriages, with all their windows closed. To my surprise, a soldier with his gun aimed at us was trembling as we boarded the carriage. He must have been worried about us attempting to escape or resisting. In this way we left Surabaya, where we had lived for some time, and began our journey without knowing our destination. As the sun was rising, a faint light filtered through gaps in the shutters, but most of the carriage was pitch-dark. I imperceptibly fell asleep on the narrow seat.

The train arrived at a station, but the guards did not allow us to open the windows. Perhaps they were afraid of us escaping, or they did not wish us to know the destination. We began talking to our neighbours in a low voice to kill time. Somehow we became cheerful, believing that we would soon be released, in spite of the fact that we were now the prisoners of enemy forces. The soldiers seemed not to have much of a presence.

The temperature inside the train rose, and it was gradually becoming hotter and more humid. As we did not have a drop of water to drink, many people began suffering from thirst. But we could do nothing about it. Fortunately, women and children were allowed to buy some drinking water, but the men had to endure thirst all day until we arrived at our destination.

The train arrived in Semarang about five hours after we boarded. We had to change to a bus from the train. Seven buses (twenty people per bus) passed through the city to a suburban area under the hot sun, and under heavy guard. As I sat in the very rear seat of the bus, I had a soldier holding a sword sitting next to me. Every time the bus swayed, his shoulder or his arm touched my body. I felt uneasy. The destination was still unknown, and no lunch had been distributed. We became despondent.

Suddenly the sky became dark, and it started raining. The bus advanced slowly, and its progress became even slower, as it had to wait for a bus following it. I became slightly irritated as many cars and taxis were swiftly overtaking us. Two hours later the bus arrived at the Ambarawa barracks and then reversed. It began moving ahead again in the heavy rain. In the bus it was getting hot and humid. The bus went over several hills and then ascended to some altitude. The scenery viewed from the window was so peaceful, with no shadow of the war to be seen. At around three o'clock in the afternoon we finally arrived at the barracks for the Sumowono firing range.

The detention camp consisted of huts built from galvanised iron sheeting, where army soldiers were billeted to practise live shooting. High mountains could be seen beyond the road, and the barracks were built on a hillslope below the road. It was a lonely place far from any human dwelling. Moreover, it was cold, as it was 1200 meters above sea level.

We passed through two checkpoints and were taken to a room that appeared to be an office. It was already after seven o'clock in the evening when we were allocated to the huts, having been divided into two groups: families and those without families. We all had sickly complexions, as we had eaten nothing since morning. We wished to eat as soon as possible, but the Dutch East Indies soldiers, who were usually not very efficient, took a long time to call the roll and to check our belongings. As there was a tap at the entrance to the hut, some people madly dashed towards it to drink water, but the guard told them not to drink the tap water, and we had no choice but to wait for the distribution of water by the army.

In the hut there were fifty shabby, wooden double-bunk beds (five shaku [about 1.5 meters] in height), and each bed was equipped with a straw mattress, two cotton blankets and a small mosquito net. The mosquito net was used not so much to repel mosquitoes, as to afford some protection from the cold air. We were thus doomed to sleep in these narrow and uncomfortable beds for the foreseeable future.

After a while, we were given a bath towel, an enamel plate, a cup, a spoon, and a fork. Now we were at least able to have a meal and a bath, though we were deprived of liberty. We were also fortunate enough to have proper bathrooms and toilets, as these were barracks for soldiers.

At around eight o'clock in the evening we were given the first meal for the day. Although the food was the same tinned rice, it was heated this time. We ate it all quickly with the fork given to us. The meal was also served with some warm water with a hint of tea colouring. We felt revived. I secretly congratulated myself, as I had endured the two most difficult days I had experienced since I was born. There were a hundred people without families in the hut to which I was allocated. After dinner, we discussed our communal life with the president of the Japan Club. We agreed that we would do our best to deal with the situation prudently. The president addressed us as follows: 'Take care of your health. No matter what has happened to us, we should not be discouraged. We must believe in the Imperial Army from the bottom of our hearts, and we must behave fairly and squarely. In so doing, we will prepare for the day of our release.'

Since I had no experience of army life, I was quite worried about participating in communal life, which I was experiencing for the first time. Nonetheless, I thought that this group situation should be a good opportunity to train myself. Once again, I vowed to do my best till the end, believing that the day of release would come soon. Thus, when I heard the signal for lights-out at nine o'clock in the evening, I welcomed the second night and laid my exhausted body down on my bed.

CHAPTER 3

SUMOWONO DETENTION CAMP DIARY

Two days had passed since the rushed arrest, and we had somehow regained a sense of calm. On 10 December we took our first steps as detainees. I shall briefly sketch how we spent our communal life day by day.

10 December 1941

I rose at around five o'clock in the morning. It was fine, in stark contrast to the bad weather the day before. I took a deep breath of fresh air and enjoyed to the full the calm and quiet scenery, far from any human dwelling. I cheered up and waited impatiently for orders from the army.

It was six o'clock in the morning ... The same tinned army food was distributed for breakfast. After breakfast, the groups for the huts were reorganised. The hundred and one male people without families were divided into four groups, with two groups occupying one hut. Each group elected a leader and each hut elected two people to liaise with the army authorities. Thus, the structure of our communal life was organised.

Then each person received a prison number instead of a private name (mine was sixty-seven). Then the blankets and other materials distributed the previous night were checked. Finally, a bed was allocated to each person.

At noon, to my surprise, rice and soup were distributed for lunch. However, this was food for prisoners. The rice was fourth-class, and contained so much grit and husk that we had to pick out these impure ingredients one by one. The soup was soup in name only, and not at all tasty. When the food was distributed, we queued up by prison number, and rice and soup were dished up into the enamel plate and cup respectively, which had been given to us the day before. At that moment, my heart was filled with deep emotion.

At half past four in the evening, dinner was distributed. It was the same as the lunch. Of course, we had to wash the dishes ourselves.

After dinner we walked in twos and threes. By seven o'clock we returned to our bed and then we had a group meeting, which bore no resemblance to a relaxed neighbourhood association meeting. At nine o'clock we went to sleep.

The regulations and routine in the detention camp were as follows:

5:30	Rise
6:30	Breakfast
11:30	Lunch
16:30	Dinner
18:00	Close windows in each hut
20:00	After this hour it was prohibited to leave the huts except to go to the toilet.
21:00	Lights out

In addition, we were not allowed to approach within a meter of the barbed wire. If a person were to approach within a meter of the barbed wire, that person would be considered to have an intention to escape and a sentry would fire his gun.

I shall describe the general condition of the Sumowono Detention Camp.

As I had already mentioned, the barracks belonged to an army live firing range. The live firing range spread from the east to the south behind the barracks, and its position was higher than the barracks. The barracks

Sumowono Barracks

1. Toilets, washrooms
   with basins, laundry
2. Interview room
3. Kitchen
4. Guard room
5. Store room
6. Sick room
7. Medical facility

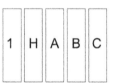

A – H Sleeping quarters

were shabby buildings made of galvanised iron sheets, located stepwise on the slope in front of the firing range. The total area of this camp was only about ten thousand square meters, and all the barracks were built facing west.

In front of the barracks we could thus see mountain after mountain stretching from the west to the north beyond the valley. In the far distance we could see Mount Sumbing and Mount Sundoro, which had a beautiful conical shape like Mount Fuji, and between the undulating mountains to the north there was a view of the sea. (The camp was about thirty kilometres south from Semarang and about sixty kilometres by road.)

Except for the area in front of each hut and the pathway between the barracks, the terrain was all rocky cliffs. Consequently, it was quite cramped. The only open space remaining was an assembly area that occupied about the same area as a barrack. Along the barbed wire surrounding the camp, five lookout points were located, and at each lookout point a sentry stood. The sentry beat an iron bar every fifteen minutes upon a signal from headquarters. We joked that this must have been done to prevent the sentry from dozing.

11 December

This morning we agreed that we would make our health our top priority for our life in the detention camp, and that we would all regularly do radio calisthenics. We immediately put this into practice, in high spirits. For breakfast, we had two slices of bread and a small amount of coffee. There was no point wishing for either butter or jam, let alone ham or sausage. It was impossible for a mortal to know that one day even such simple food as bread and coffee would become a luxury. After breakfast, we washed our underwear. Because we did not have soap, we just rinsed them with water. We had no spare underwear and no choice but to use the towel distributed the day before to wrap around our body. For lunch, we had a piece of boiled and seasoned tofu, soup, and rice. As the tofu was seasoned with neither soy sauce nor sugar, we had little appetite for it. We had little chance of enjoying any vegetables or fruit. I wished for just a piece of yellow pickled radish or pickled plum.

For dinner, the same food was distributed as the day before. We ate only to satisfy our hunger. I was struck by the realisation that my fortunate life prior to my arrest had left me unprepared to endure life in detention.

12 December

We decided that the radio calisthenics, which we all agreed to do together, should be done by each group separately, as we did not wish to provoke the army authorities. On this day we had tobacco distributed for the first time, and the smokers were delighted.

13 December

We received twenty cents as an allowance for the four days from 9 to 12 December, which was almost all appropriated to pay for the tobacco distributed the day before. The remaining money was to be used to jointly purchase laundry soap. For dinner, we had mangos for the first time, but we could not eat them because of their bad odour.

14 December

As new detainees would be arriving this morning, all male people without families were reunited and allocated to one hut.

For dinner, bananas were distributed, and we were able to enjoy fruit for the first time in a while.

15 December

At around eight o'clock in the morning, a group of a little more than two hundred people detained in Semarang arrived under guard from the Ambarawa barracks. The guard was extremely strict as usual, and we were cooped up in the hut. Although I tried to observe the movement of the group from the window, I could not see clearly due to the distance. With some difficulty I recognised a person who looked like Mr Sasamura, the branch manager of the Yokohama Specie Bank from Semarang, but I could not see Mr Nakata, the deputy branch manager. (Later I found out that Mr Nakata had gone on a business trip to Batavia and that he was detained there.) In due course, when the group had been checked and sent to the hut, I met with Mr Sasamura. We were glad that we were both unhurt, and we talked about how we were arrested.

At around six o'clock in the evening, six people were brought to the camp from Lombok Island. According to the information that these people heard from the guards, the fall of the Philippines and Singapore was imminent, and Moscow had fallen on 8 December. (I thought that this news seemed unlikely to be true.)

On the other hand, according to news from the Dutch East Indies army, our Imperial Army had shot down five hundred American combat planes in Hawaii. We were also informed of the attack on American warships at Pearl Harbor.

16 December

All day we were troubled by the sound of the rain blowing against our hut.

17 December

In the afternoon, our group from Surabaya played baseball, the old people playing against the young people. It must have been funny to look at, as we hit a ball-like object, which we made very quickly, with a cudgel. It was still an enjoyable thing to do to kill time. We all played with enthusiasm, and everyone participated actively as if we had become children again. The score was 6 to 1, the young group winning by five points. Today we received a toothbrush, toothpaste, and bath soap, which we waited for impatiently. These goods were bought with money borrowed from the people taken from Semarang. We were able to clean our teeth properly and had a bath using bath soap for the first time in ten days. (Our group from Surabaya could not bring any money with us, as all our money was confiscated when we were arrested.)

18 December

Today I was on food distribution duty for the first time. I got up at around four o'clock in the morning. After waiting for dawn to break, I made my way to the cookhouse. Although stars were still shining in the sky, its eastern fringe was dyed with crimson. My field of vision gradually opened up, and the mountains emerged from the mist. When the beautiful shapes of Mt Sumbing and Mt Sundoro appeared in the distance, illuminated by the morning sun, I felt as if I was looking at a fine scroll. The Sumowono mountains behind them appeared to be still asleep. It was the best time of the day, and I was absorbed in the scenery, which kept changing its shape and colour every minute.

Soon, at six o'clock in the morning, those rostered on food duty received bread and coffee from the cookhouse, delivered it to his or her hut, and distributed it. After breakfast, each group began cleaning their hut with a broom or a rag. Even those who had never used a broom in the outside world had to participate in cleaning. I was quite sorry to see them working awkwardly with their broom. In the detention camp everyone was equal, and nobody could escape their duties. However, everyone was different, and everyone's capacity had its limitations. Elderly and disabled people needed to be treated differently. Children and women also had clear limitations in their capacity for physical work. Therefore, in a spirit of mutual aid, they were excluded from cleaning.

On the other hand, apart from those of us from mainland Japan, people of Taiwanese and Chinese nationality, and Javanese people, were also detained. Consequently, some racial issues arose, as their manners and customs were different to ours. Some misunderstandings also occurred between us. In this way, a dark shadow was cast over our future. It was inevitable that those from mainland Japan should set some clear rules according to their moral judgement, but this was not sufficient. As those from mainland Japan were in a majority, we felt obliged to show some leadership. At the same time, we should not have excluded people of other nationalities. This was what I strongly felt at the time.

When we were about to prepare for dinner, a group of people left behind in eastern Java were escorted to the camp in ten buses. There were about three hundred people in total, and most of them were women and children of Taiwanese nationality. Amongst them there were young children carried by their mothers. The news from the leader of the group that our army was superior to the enemy added to our happiness. On the other hand, all sorts of false news was flying around as usual.

20 December
Every day was much the same. Although we made a big effort to do washing, there were frequent showers, as often happens in the highlands,

and the washing did not dry as we wished. However, I was delighted when I had a change of clothes that were borrowed from newcomers to the camp. I was also able to borrow a needle and some thread from the women's group. I was extremely happy when, with a shaky hand, I somehow managed to mend my trousers myself. As my hair and beard had grown freely, my features had changed completely.

We were informed that a canteen would be opening in a few days, but that was of little interest to those of us who had no money. The food was much the same every day: rice and a side dish, with no vegetables or fruit. The number of people currently detained was about six hundred in total. We were divided into six huts: three huts for male people without families and three huts for families. Although some people wished to subscribe to a newspaper or a journal, they were not allowed to do so. It was lucky that some old newspapers and journals, which were smuggled in, were circulated for everyone to read.

Anyway, we had plenty of time to kill, and fretted about our forced idleness. Today we were formally informed of new camp rules:

5:30 Rise at bugle call

5:45 Roll call, making beds, cleaning

6:00 Group leader to report the roll call to the army authorities and inform them if anyone is sick.

6:15 Any sick person to be examined in the dispensary.

6:30 Breakfast preparation

7:00 ~ 10:00 Free time (Requests to be proposed in writing through the group leader by eight o'clock.)

11:15 Roll call in rooms

11:30 Lunch preparation

1:00 ~ 4:00 Free time

4:15 Roll call

4:30 Dinner preparation

5:00 ~ 8:30 Free time

9:30　　Lights out

Every Saturday the dirt floor should be cleaned.

On Sunday, rise at 6 and roll to be called at 6:15.

In addition, when an air raid alarm sounded, everyone should stand in front of their bed.

21 December

This morning there was no bugle call. It was not clear whether this was caused by the laziness of the soldier. We had a *shōgi* [Japanese chess] tournament. Those of us from the Surabaya group played against the allies from eastern Java ... The Surabaya group won all games.

22 December

At eleven o'clock in the morning we all observed a moment of silence when the body of an eight-month-old baby girl of Chinese nationality, who died the day before, was carried out.

The detainees received five cents per day, the same as the army soldiers did. This amount of money was not directly given to us, as all our money was pooled to buy our necessities, which were distributed to us later according to our need. On the other hand, those who deposited currency at the time of detention were allowed to withdraw two guilders and fifty cents per week. However, the canteen had not yet opened, so they could not do anything with that money.

Today the soldiers had live shooting practice, and the sound of gunfire could be heard in the distance.

23 December

At eight o'clock in the morning Mr Togami and I were summoned to the office, but we were mistaken for staff from Nan'yō Sōko.[1]

1　Nan'yō Sōko was a Japanese warehouse company established in Taipei in 1912.

24 December

I was busy with food duty. Recently people of Chinese and Taiwanese nationality have fallen sick one after another, as they suffer from malnutrition caused by an unbalanced diet.

A Taiwanese person aged 44 died.

25 December

Although today was Christmas day, our life remained much the same. Some people from the Surabaya group received a half-sleeve shirt and shorts made for prisoners. Because of our poor diet, our talk about food became animated. We talked about home culinary specialties of which we were proud. At ten o'clock in the morning we observed a minute of silence for the person who had died the day before. In the afternoon, several new Chinese and local detainees were brought to the camp.

26 December

A half-sleeve shirt and shorts for prisoners were distributed to those from the Surabaya group who did not receive them the day before. These clothes were a poor fit, but thanks to them I was now able to wash the white clothes which I had been wearing since my arrest.

Our request for us to be allocated to different huts according to our nationality was granted. Now that we could stay in different huts, we could avoid the troubles caused by having different habits and customs.

27 December

This was a big cleaning day. We disinfected all rooms, and all our bedding was disinfected by placing it in the sun. We heard news that our Imperial Army had landed on the eastern part of Sumatra and part of Borneo. We agreed that we would sleep in our prisoners' clothes from now on, to prepare for any emergency.

28 December

From this night on we decided to observe the movements of the guard by appointing a night watchman. At the same time, each of us was allotted a role in our emergency procedures, and we agreed that everyone would act with discipline under the command of our leader.

I was allocated to a group to destroy the barbed wire. We were ordered to stand a table against the barbed wire and open an escape point. The plan was first to escape by breaking through a point that was poorly guarded, even if we had some casualties. Then those who succeeded in escaping would initiate a guerrilla war in liaison with our army or with Javanese people. However, we had no weapons to fight with. I had grave doubts whether we could fight against the guards. I thought that this would be rather reckless. The leaders of this plan were officials who used to serve in the army. Theirs was just a plan invented by old officials with little hope of success, and it was indeed reckless. However, this plan was made on condition that the number of guards would be about twenty with one machine gun. Later we learnt that there were many more guards and weapons than we anticipated. It was lucky that we did not go ahead with this plan.

29 December

I was on food duty. As the end of the year was approaching, we heatedly debated whether we would be released by the first of January or not. At noon, the news broke that our army had issued an ultimatum to the Dutch East Indies government. At around half past seven in the evening, an air raid alarm was given for the first time. Everyone became tense, but an all clear was given twenty minutes later. This was a military exercise, but we felt that the time for battle was quickly approaching.

30 December

At two o'clock in the afternoon all three of us from the Surabaya group were called into the office. We were asked about the lock for the safe in our branch and about the combination for the lock. About eight o'clock in the evening a rumour passed around that our army had landed on both the east and west coasts of Java. The three of us from the Yokohama Specie Bank were on night watch duty.

31 December

Today marked the end of the year 1941.

On the notice board in the cookhouse the number of detainees in each hut was posted. According to this notice, each hut had the following number of occupants:

A: 103 people

B: 95 people

C: 101 people

D: 100 people

E: 67 people

F: 99 people

G: 29 people

H: 74 people

I: 43 people

J: 10 people

Total: 721 people

This left a surplus detention capacity of about 130 people. At ten o'clock in the morning a roll call of all detainees was conducted, and sixty cents daily allowance that had not been distributed was handed out. (PS: The numbers for huts 'I' and 'J' are provisional.)

In the afternoon it rained heavily. Sadly, we spent the last day of the year in prison. I prayed at the end of the year: 'Glory to my motherland!'

1 January

Having greeted the first day of the new year, I prayed for long life for the Emperor and celebrated the prosperity of the royal family. I also celebrated the prosperity of my country and prayed for continuing good fortune in battle for each soldier on the front line. From that remote place I prayed that the souls of those soldiers who died to protect our country might rest in peace. I also paid respect from the bottom of my heart to those women who put up a good fight. We all prayed that we would be released as soon as possible. We vowed to each other that once we were released, we would sincerely serve our country, each in our own occupation, and would repay our debt to the Emperor.

However, we refrained from having a minute's silence to show our gratitude towards the soldiers of the Imperial Army, and from making a bow towards the Imperial Palace. As almost all the news received till today had no clear source, we supposed that this news might be a prank played by the guards. Today we also received news that a convoy of sixty Japanese ships departing from Singapore had been attacked by a Dutch East Indies submarine and that nine of them had sunk. Presumably, this was enemy propaganda. Anyway, I thought that the Dutch East Indies campaign by our army was about to start.

Today windowpanes in the huts were all painted a dark purple colour as the part of the air defence preparations. Light bulbs were painted the same colour.

2 January

I became aware that a billiard room had been open since the end of the previous year, but it was open in name only. In actual fact, we could not use it.

According to the rules, it was permitted to read journals and newspapers, but there was nothing like a journal or newspaper to be found. The request to open a canteen had been granted, but it was just a verbal promise. The canteen had not yet opened.

3 January

According to a newspaper which I obtained on this day, our army's attack against Manila and Hawaii was reported as follows in news from America and England:

(1) Five warships sank, beginning with the American warship *Arizona*, which was anchored at Pearl Harbor at that time and many fighter planes on the land were destroyed. This attack appeared to have been made by

squadrons of fighter planes from more than three aircraft carriers of the Japanese Navy. The article also dealt with the activities of small two-man submarines.

(2) Off the coast of Manila, the Allies had hit the Japanese warship *Harina* with three bombs.

(3) At sea near Singapore, the English warship *Prince of Wales* and one other warship [*Repulse*] were bombed and sunk.

In total three hundred Chinese and local people detained here were to be transferred to a different camp. Ten buses and three trucks which would escort them arrived at around five o'clock in the afternoon.

4 January

It was discovered that some people secretly possessed silver coins. We were informed that from now on if a person possessed more than three hundred guilders in cash, this money would be confiscated. This had nothing to do with those of us in the group from Surabaya. This morning the Chinese and some other people were transferred out, and the number of people detained became as follows:

A: 98 people

B: 48 people

C: 88 people

D: 100 people

E: 66 people

F: 99 people

G: 15 people

H: 20 people

I: 38 people

J: 9 people

Total: 581 people.

After some time, just one plane flew over the camp. This suggested that our army had not landed on Java. That night, I was on night watch duty.

5 January

Before breakfast, someone told us that he read a newspaper article about the fall of Singapore and the start of the Australian campaign. Once again, we were not sure whether it was true or not. Although it appeared that the Southward campaign[2] was about to start, I felt that Java had been left alone. It was possible that Java would be occupied by Japan without bloodshed. Then our release would be delayed, but it would be inevitable.

A rumour spread that the Chinese and the other people who had left the day before were taken to a prison in Bandung. It was not at all clear whether this was true or not. Today was another day when rumours were flying around.

6 January

The canteen was expected to open in the billiard room, which had been open for a while, but food would be excluded from the goods sold here. From 10 o'clock we were once again interrogated about our address, occupation, and place of arrest. As we had already been interrogated about these matters several times, we were not convinced of the necessity for such interrogation. In addition, we were ordered to return some military currency, that had been distributed earlier, to the military authorities. They would be entrusted to the army authorities.

At around half past seven, we were suddenly ordered to retire to our huts and remain there quietly. We stood in front of each bed for about thirty minutes, and then the alert was cancelled. Presumably, it was an emergency drill.

7 January

At around six o'clock in the morning a group of soldiers in several trucks arrived at the camp. Soon after that, the sound of rifles and pistols resounded in the Sumowono mountains, which were quiet following

---

2 The 'Southward campaign' is more commonly referred to in English language sources as the 'South East Asian campaign'.

some rain. The soldiers fired five times each, and the live firing exercise finished after about one hour. Meanwhile, ten or so soldiers carried out a military drill on the parade ground. They appeared to be new recruits, as they wore poorly fitting military uniforms, and they had a gas mask and a small rucksack on their back. It was particularly noticeable that they had a spoon stuck in their puttees. Although the Junior Lieutenant instructing them proudly ordered them about, the soldiers' drill was worse than that of high school students in Japan. In the huts we started making *Ogura Hyakunin Isshu* [one hundred people, one poem each] cards.[3] At around four o'clock in the evening one hundred and twelve Japanese people transferred from Manado arrived at the camp. They had boarded a ship at a port on the eastern coast of Celebes on 30 December. They were locked up in the hold. They did not have a proper toilet, let alone a bath. They had had been poorly treated. This morning they landed on Surabaya and were then brought to this camp by the same route as we had been. The group included old people, women, and children. Luckily, they did not have any casualties, but they all had sickly complexions. They were utterly exhausted. Our group straight away gathered left-over rice and made several rice balls. When we presented them to the people from Manado, they were moved to tears, saying, 'what warm brotherly love!'

8 January

This morning we visited the hut where the people from Manado were detained. We heard from the leader of the group about what occurred after their arrest. The story we heard was as follows:

> We were in prison for two weeks from 8 December. We received no blanket and slept on the floor. While we ate bread for breakfast and dinner, we had rice for lunch. Fortunately, we were able to buy some food with help from the local guards. We just managed to survive.

---

3   A popular card game known as *Uta-garuta* made use of cards with quotations from classical poems written on them. The game was especially popular during New Year celebrations.

On 26 December we saw our military planes begin bombing. When we saw with our own eyes how our planes swooped down to bomb, we were greatly encouraged.

However, the Dutch East Indies government sensed danger, and transferred us to the mountains, about two hundred and twenty kilometres away from the prison. Three days later they transferred us again to a different location. Then, we were squeezed onto an old bus. The bus was repeatedly brought to a standstill due to engine failure. After undergoing repairs several times, the bus finally arrived at our destination at two o'clock in the morning on the following day. At five o'clock, without any sleep, we were transferred to the eastern coast by bus, and forced on board a ship.

Thus, our stressful life in the narrow hold of the ship began. We felt more dead than alive. As the entrance was shut, the inside of the ship was hot and humid. On top of that, there was no toilet. We had to use buckets to urinate and defecate. Then we had to lift the buckets up to the deck to empty them. This operation was extremely difficult, as the ship often pitched and rolled.

The ship finally entered a port in Makassar on 2 January, but we were not able to disembark. We were taken to Surabaya, where we disembarked early in the morning on 7 January. We felt relieved, but soon after that we were forced to go on a train. Luckily, we were able to buy food freely on the train.

That was what we heard from the leader of the group. Moreover, we heard that both Surabaya and Semarang remained calm and peaceful. It turned out that almost all the news we had heard till now was false rumours.

After breakfast we received a transfer order. We gathered our belongings as we waited for departure. Of course, our destination was unknown. After lunch, bread and an oil drum containing coffee prepared for us were loaded on the truck, but there were no signs of departure. At around two o'clock in the afternoon the leader of the Manado group came to say farewell to us. They asked whether they could see our group off or not. We turned down their offer, as we did not know the departure time.

And so, both the remaining and the departing groups stood in line in front of their huts and exchanged parting words. Those who were remaining and those who were departing were all in tears and reluctant to part. The time went by, but nobody wanted to leave, as everyone was in the same boat. We did not know what would happen on the morrow. Viewing the situation from the point of view of the people from Manado, they were finally united with us after a difficult journey, and then they had to be separated from us in less than a day. They thought that we shared the fate of being captured in a remote country far away from the motherland, and that we would now be able to console each other, but ... Finally, we decided to return to our huts, as they could not stop lamenting our departure. Then they also decided to return to their huts. What a beautiful brotherly love they showed to us. We all burst into tears at that point, as we felt that they were a godsend to us in our hardship.

Just then, the sky suddenly became overcast, and big drops of rain started falling. We felt as if the sky sympathised with us and shed tears with us. The beat of the rain gradually quickened, and the temperature in the highlands suddenly dropped. At about three o'clock in the afternoon some rice balls were kindly sent from the group from Manado in return for our present of the day before. We were all very moved.

At around four o'clock in the afternoon we received the departure order, as the rain eased.

Those of us in the group from Surabaya marched at the head as we left the detention camp where we had lived for about a month. First, we were divided into groups of twenty people. Then they checked our names, and we went on twenty-seven buses which had been arranged for us. It took more than two hours for about six hundred of us to board the buses, and as usual we were strictly guarded. The number of guards was more than we expected, with two soldiers being allocated to the front and back entrances of each bus, ominously pointing the muzzles of their guns at us. The atmosphere in the bus was gloomy, as we all kept silent, but as time went by we started talking each other.

So it was that, at a quarter past six in the evening, the long line of prison buses began moving, guided by a motorbike with sidecar. The dusk gathered and the Sumowono mountains were covered by thick rain clouds. We felt that it was hard to leave.

The buses moved slowly through hills along the narrow road. What attracted our attention was that all the houses were painted with the air defence colour. We were surprised that the wartime hue had penetrated even into such remote countryside.

By the time the buses were approaching the foot of the mountain, the rain had stopped, but it was getting humid inside the buses as the windows were all shut. Night fell, and the buses moved through the darkness with their headlights on. At around eight o'clock in the evening the buses entered the town of Magelang, where a blackout was in place, and we could see nothing of the state of the town. The buses stopped for about thirty minutes, but we could not get out of the bus, even to go to the lavatory.

Soon the headlights were turned off and the buses began moving again. At around ten o'clock in the evening we arrived at Jogja Station. We were immediately transferred onto the carriages of a special train (fourth-class carriages with nailed down windows). We had only one small candle to light the carriage, and sixty-two people were crammed into that poorly lit space. When we sat down on three long wooden benches, we were relieved. We had managed to travel from the cool highlands for four hours, fighting against the heat and drowsiness. We had also been transferred from a cramped bus to the carriage of a train. We felt like little birds transferred from a small cage to a large one. We stretched ourselves, like birds spreading their wings.

Guards were posted at the front and back entrances of the carriages, and then the coffee prepared for us was finally distributed to our teacups, but our teacups were only half filled. However, we had not yet had any of the bread prepared for dinner.

At around fifty minutes past midnight on 9 January, the train finally began advancing towards the west. As the carriage swayed violently, it was difficult to fall asleep. Although we anticipated that we might be talking to each other all through the night, people fell asleep one after another due to exhaustion. The sounds of snoring could be heard from all over the carriage. The candle was extinguished without anyone noticing, and the interior of the carriage was dimly illuminated by moonlight shining through the shutters. I also fell asleep, taking care to protect myself from the cold dawn air. When I woke up, it was two o'clock in the morning, and the train was advancing due west. As dawn approached, we suffered from the cold air. It became difficult for me to fall asleep. Moreover, I felt hungry, as since lunch the previous day I had eaten only the single rice ball given to us by the people from Manado.

When dawn broke, the train was still advancing to the west. As we could not recognise the names of the stations that the train passed through, our destination was still unknown. At eight o'clock in the morning we were finally given the bread we had been waiting for so impatiently, but no water was distributed. As the sun was rising higher, it was again getting hot in the carriage. A person who was familiar with western Java told us that we had just passed through Cikampek Station. Perhaps we would travel on to either Galu or Sukabumi via Batavia Station, although it was a detour. Then we would be united with people detained in Western Java.

At about ten o'clock the train arrived at Batavia Station, and then it seemed to reverse direction. This reinforced the view that our destination could be Galu.

However, as the train was running on rusty rails, a person who had lived in Batavia for a long time drew the conclusion that this must be the incoming line from Priok. As expected, our prisoner-train stopped at a wharf. We immediately became tense, as now we knew that we were doomed to be transferred by ship to an unknown destination. At noon, we were ordered to get off the train. We passed in front of a shed belonging to KPM [a Dutch shipping company] and then arrived in the entrance of the customs house. First, we had a rollcall of names, and then we passed through an interview room one by one. We stood in line on the wharf where a ship marked 'Cremer' was anchored, and they started checking our belongings under the burning sun.

On both sides of the passage from the building of the customs house to the *Cremer*, apart from the armed soldiers, police officers, KPM office workers, and lowly ranked sailors were standing threateningly with bayonets, long swords, pistols and other arms in their hands. We calmly marched in front of them and waited for an hour in the direct sunshine until they finished checking our belongings.

Our group was to board the *Cremer*, which carried both cargo and passengers, with a gross tonnage of seven thousand tons. We were taken into the dark rear of the hold. As all the windows were welded, we could not see outside. On the deck there was no carpet. Although we tried to sit down, it was not comfortable to do so. It was so cramped that each person had just enough room to lie down. Bravo, we had become deck passengers!

At the entrance to the hold a machine gun was pointing its ominous muzzle at us through wire netting. (This ship later became known as a hell ship.) First, we spread our cotton blanket distributed to us at the Sumowono camp on the deck ... With this blanket we had wrapped our plate and cup and other things to carry with us while we were moving. We never thought that this blanket would become our carpet.

At about three o'clock in the afternoon a group of people from western Java, about three hundred from the Galu detention camp, were transferred to join us. Having arrived earlier, we went out to greet them. Those who worked for the Yokohama Specie Bank took some time to emerge. I heard people come out by alphabetical order. First Mr Kuriyama, then

Mr Matsumoto and Mr Nakata came out, and then Mr Sakimura and Mr Sunami followed, and finally Mr Taketani appeared. It took nearly one hour to see everyone from the Yokohama Specie Bank. Everyone was sunburnt, and I found it difficult to recognise them. Presumably, they must have been surprised when they saw me, as my complexion was totally changed.

The people from Galu were sent to the hold below ours. In that hold some of the people from Sumatra had already boarded. According to them, we were transferred to be exchanged. I still could not understand the need for such an extremely strict guard but was not overly concerned about it.

Soon the ship began sailing smoothly westwards. The time was half past four in the afternoon. It was hard for everyone to find his or her own spot, as the detainees numbered nearly one thousand. The people from Galu were not allowed to carry a blanket with them, so those of us from Surabaya shared our blankets with them. When the sun set, dinner was prepared at around seven o'clock in the evening. We queued up, one group at a time, and received rice, two pieces of tinned sardine, and a cup of warm water.

Everyone seemed happy, as they satisfied their empty stomach. We were particularly glad to have some fish for the first time during our detention. (However, we gradually grew bored with the same menu again and again during the voyage.) After finishing our feast, we began preparing for sleep. We had no blanket to cover ourselves, let alone a pillow or pyjamas. We had no choice but to lie down with just what we wore. As it was hot and humid, it was difficult to go to sleep. Nevertheless, at around eight o'clock some people fell asleep, as they were exhausted by the long journey that had commenced the day before.

CHAPTER 4

MEMOIR OF THE VOYAGE TO AUSTRALIA ON BOARD THE *CREMER*

I shall write a memoir about our twenty-day voyage from 9 January 1942, the day when, under strict guard, we were forced to board the *Cremer*, which belonged to KPM. It seemed to us during the voyage that we were living through hell.

From the time the ship sailed from Batavia until she called into Cilacap, she endlessly changed direction, first to the north, then to the south, and then to the east. Consequently, we had absolutely no idea where we were being transported to. At first, most of us thought that we were sailing on the Indian Ocean, judging by the ocean swell. However, the ship just kept sailing at a decent speed without us sighting any island for three days. Once we thought that we might be being transported to Sumatra, but some thought that we were being taken to Celebes. As the ship kept changing direction, we could not guess where we were going. Because the portholes were all covered by iron plates, we could just see the surface of the sea through tiny chinks. The portholes may have been covered to protect against attack by our Imperial Army. It was unfortunate for us that the ship did not carry Red Cross markings. The ship might have been attacked at any time by the Japanese armed forces. We tried hard to find a way to let the Japanese armed forces know that this ship carried some Japanese, but we could do nothing. I stayed in Surabaya until the last moment in the hope that I could do something for the Japanese empire, even though my ability was limited. The thought that I might be drowned at sea vexed me. I could only pray for the gods and Buddha to protect me, so that I could survive and render some last service to my country.

We all spent days absolutely without hope, but the ship finally called in to Cilacap, which was the first and the last port of call in Java. We also learned that this ship was going to Australia, judging from the cargo that was loaded. In passing, I shall mention the issue of drinking water. As soon as we went on board, we asked for some drinking water. We were told that we should drink water from taps set in two places in the hold. Although we were extremely happy when we were given some warm drinking water on the first night after boarding, we had to drink cold water from the following day onwards. We felt it extremely important to secure drinking water while the ship was at sea, and we needed to manage the use of water ourselves. Some members of our group voluntarily took responsibility to look after the hold on the first floor. Thereafter, we informed everyone that while we would use only seawater for washing clothes, for the time being we would supply one cup of water each morning to wash our face and one cup of water for each meal. However, we had no way of enforcing our request, and some people in our group carelessly used drinking water for washing clothes or bathing. We had to convince all our group that we needed to save our precious water while the ship was at sea. We asked everyone to exercise self-control in using drinking water and we did strictly observe our rules. Our efforts were not in vain, and we were able to make our drinking water last till the end of the voyage. I was delighted that we could maintain our supply, even though its amount was extremely limited towards the end. Indeed, when the voyage was nearly over, the amount of drinking water was at a dangerous level, and at one stage we were blamed for it. In the end, we felt satisfied with all the measures we had taken.

Next, I shall talk about food distribution. Although we organised a food distribution group and tried to administer the distribution of food smoothly, some group members acted selfishly. It cast some doubt on our future communal life. Because we, the Japanese nation, as leaders of the East Asian countries, were destined to embrace and guide many other nations whose manners and customs were different to ours, we felt an urgent need to think about the best way to conduct our communal life.

I shall also write about our diet. Every day we were given much the same food, as follows:

Breakfast: soup with green beans (about two tablespoons), coffee, dried fish, and rice.

Lunch: an exceedingly small amount of beef soup, meat with bones that might have been used to make soup stock, and rice (occasionally a duck egg).

Dinner: a piece of tinned sardine (sometimes two pieces), soup with red pepper and rice.

Such was the menu, and there was much more variety in the food supplied at the Sumowono detention camp. Although we had no hope of receiving fresh fruit and vegetables, fortunately no one suffered from malnutrition while we were on board.

Incidentally, we all had dark and sickly complexions. This may have been caused by a lack of bathing.

Regrettably, some people in our group began pestering the guards to give them tobacco and sweets. Although thoughtful and sensible people deplored their actions, we could not stop them doing so. Apart from this, it is worth mentioning that mothers with unweaned babies requested the distribution of powdered milk. Although it took a while for their requests to be satisfied, they finally received some powdered milk because of persistent efforts.

After leaving Cilacap, the further the ship advanced towards the south, the colder it became. It was especially difficult when our dreams were often broken by seawater entering the ship over the gunwale.

We had become so accustomed to the warm climate in Java, a land of perpetual summer. When the cold air mass from the Antarctic Pole hit us, we just shivered, as we lacked any winter clothing. It was particularly difficult during the night, as we had no proper bedding. Sometimes we could not get to sleep until morning, trying to avoid the cold wind blowing onto the deck.

Moreover, there were no medical supplies, even when someone fell sick. When many people suffered from diarrhoea, we could not isolate them. We could do nothing but gather those who suffered from diarrhoea near the toilet. The deck was packed to overflowing with people. And then the ship began pitching and rolling badly. We could not clean the toilet and its stench filled the whole ship. On top of that, most people were unable to have a proper bath for so long that an odd smell permeated the hold. It seemed as if we were living through hell.

As we were on a ship, we could not wash our clothes as we wished. It was even more difficult for the mothers with infants to wash clothes. Our situation was such that I could not fully describe the hardship experienced by everyone. Two people died from sickness during the voyage, and we had to bury those bodies in the Indian Ocean. They received neither treatment nor medication. A young Dutch East Indies officer used abusive language: 'We will be annoyed if you escape, but we do not mind if you die from sickness.' We began wondering whether these officers could show any sign of humanity. Even though we were people from an enemy country, we were not prisoners of war, but internees. Therefore, we firmly protested the inhumane treatment of patients to the army authority, and we requested an improvement in the treatment of sick people.

I thought I would bide my time. Then I would appeal to the whole world and ask the officers of the Dutch East Indies to take responsibility for their deeds. Souls of the dead, please rest in peace ... I pray with my hands folded ...

Since we had been interned, we had had no chance to taste anything sweet. One day we happened to receive one piece of biscuit. We divided it into twelve so that everyone could enjoy it. The piece of biscuit reminded us of life in Java. We wished for just a piece of bread with some butter or jam.

One more thing that made us uneasy was the way local soldiers on patrol would threateningly swing their swords as if wielding the green dragon sabre. If the ship had rolled, anything could have happened. We were also annoyed by the soldiers humming or talking loudly at night. When we asked them to stop doing so, they began jeering vulgarly. Their jeering was so loud that we could not sleep.

We believed that the gods would bring down a hammer on their heads and prayed solely for a safe voyage.

From now on, I shall write a diary day by day.

10 January 1942

We greeted the first morning after boarding. The ship was extremely crowded, with people rushing around in utter confusion. Although we were interned, it was such a bright morning. Although we could not erase our anxiety and did not know where we were going, we prayed that we would arrive at our destination as soon as possible. 'Danger past, God forgotten', as the saying goes. We were very conscious of human weakness.

I heard children cry somewhere in the distance. On the ship many people were busy chatting loudly. It had been decided that food would be distributed to groups of twenty persons. Our group from the Sumowono detention camp once again organised several groups and asked young volunteers to be on duty for food distribution. This was because people began collapsing one after another due to seasickness, as the ship had rolled badly during the preceding night.

Although the ship at first headed in a north-westerly direction, it seemed to have changed direction to the east. Then we became aware that the ship was changing direction to the south. We had absolutely no idea what our destination was.

People conjectured that our destination could be Australia, Sumatra, or Celebes. We spent a long time arguing endlessly about our destination. Guard-soldiers patrolled from time to time, day and night. Every soldier with a drawn sword looked frightening. They appeared to be saying, if you come closer to me, I will behead you with this sword.

11 January 1942

The ship pitched and rolled badly due to the heavy swell on the Indian Ocean. In the afternoon we were hit by a squall, and rain came into the hold. It was all we could do to shelter from it. We could not wash our clothes as we wished. Consequently, underclothes soiled with sweat were piled up at the head of our beds.

12 January 1942

From early morning we argued heatedly about our destination. We were informed that part of an island was sighted around eight o'clock in the morning. We peered intently through a crack in the iron sheeting covering the portholes. Some said that we were entering a port in the east of Java, while others said that we were entering an army port newly built on the island of Celebes. While we were arguing, the ship was approaching the port, where weird, dark green seawater lay stagnant. It was around ten o'clock. We noticed several trucks were moving along a road near the coast. The ship stopped and we were told that she would be anchored all day today. Those who were suffering from seasickness felt relieved when they heard this. A roll call, conducted by gender, began at around eleven o'clock in the morning. Perhaps they were attempting to segregate family groups.

In the afternoon, barbed wire was put up at the cargo delivery entrance on the upper deck, and cargo loading began.

At around eleven o'clock at night, heavy rain descended on us. The rain fell mercilessly into the delivery entrance and we were deprived of a place to sleep. We were bewildered.

13 January 1942

It appeared that the ship would be at anchor all day again.

Before noon, they checked the gender of minors. The temperature in the ship had risen rapidly and it became very hot and humid. People became sick one after another and some suffered from diarrhoea. We became anxious. Fortunately, a sanitary group was organised with a doctor on board as the head. The patients were examined, but there was no medication available. Hence, no treatment was given. The only thing we could do was to use disinfectant to prevent new cases of diarrhoea.

Cargo loading began in the dark at around ten o'clock at night. The shadows of coolies could be seen on the deck. As I could not go to sleep due to the heat, I watched the coolies handling the cargo. The combination of the loud noise from the crane and the high-pitched voices of the coolies became unbearable.

There was no way of knowing the content of the cargo. The cargo loading finished in about one hour. I heard some guards whistling or humming in the distance from the upper deck.

In the sky bright stars were shining.

14 January 1942

I must have fallen asleep despite the hot and humid night. I was woken by the shouting of sailors.

From early morning many people began going back and forth through the passage near our beds to wash clothes or have a bath. Then some people began fetching drinking water. It was so noisy that I could not stay in bed, so I got up at around four o'clock in the morning and volunteered to fetch drinking water for the group.

After breakfast, the cargo loading resumed. As we saw cargo such as brandy and tea being loaded for Australia and New Zealand, we thought that the ship must be heading for Australia. We all agreed that the port where the ship was anchored was Cilacap. It was difficult for us to correctly guess where we were, as even those who had lived there for more than twenty years could not see a full view of the port.

The sun shone directly on the ship, and inside the ship became a melting pot. Consequently, many people wanted to drink water. Those distributing drinking water became extremely busy.

Cargo loading continued in the afternoon. It was slowly getting cooler inside the ship as evening approached. We had a little relief, but then a squall hit us. We did our best to take refuge from it. We wrapped up all our belongings with the cotton blanket which we used for bedding and climbed to a safe place, like refugees from an earthquake. We waited for the rain to stop, then we wiped the wet floor with towels and rested on our dry cotton blankets.

We requested the army authority to cover the cargo delivery entrance with waterproof cloth. Although the rain stopped coming in, it became extremely hot, like a sauna, inside the ship, as a vent had been covered. We now had to ask the army authority to remove the waterproof cloth. The soldier on duty ignored our request, and we had to put up with the situation.

Every time I heard children cry due to the hot and humid conditions, I was moved to tears.

A rumour spread that VIPs in the government, starting with the Governor General and their family, had boarded to escape from the war to Australia.

Next, the distribution of tobacco, which we had been requesting for a while, was denied. As the number of patients with a high fever had increased, we requested medical supplies. This was denied as well. We all agreed to pay more attention to our health, and we also decided to clean the toilet twice a day.

15 January 1942
As the ship did not have enough ventilation, a strange odour of perspiration and toilet stench filled the ship.

Around seven o'clock in the morning the rain stopped, and the cover of the delivery entrance was taken off. We felt revived. Because those who could not sleep all night, due to the wet floor, began using the tap water before dawn, we too ended up not sleeping all night. The number of people washing their underwear also increased. Not the flags of all nations, but many clothes, were hanging all over the deck. At around four o'clock in the afternoon the cargo loading was finally completed, and the ship began to move. We were, of course, not informed where the ship was heading. We thought that the voyage would take a long time, as we had seen several cows hitched at a corner of the upper deck the previous night. We guessed that these cows would be slaughtered for eating during the voyage. Of course, this would be done not for us but for white people who were on board.

Our group from Surabaya included two patients with high fever. Other groups also had several people with high fever. The number of patients had reached more than ten. We tried to isolate them, but there was no place to put them. We had no choice but to place them in front of the toilet, which was located at the very rear of the hold. We also instructed everyone to use disinfectant thoroughly, so that we could stop the outbreak of an epidemic.

Although more than a week had already passed since we boarded, we had not had any fruit or fresh vegetables. On top of this, we did not get enough exercise. We were quite worried about the increase in the number of sick people, but we could not do anything to stop it. The hot and humid nights continued. The ship was smoothly ploughing through the waves of the Indian Ocean.

This morning we heard that almost seven hundred people, who had been detained on Borneo and Celebes, were on board the ship. We also heard that Mr Imagawa (the former general manager of the Yokohama branch of the Special Bank of Java, who had been detained at Medan on his way home to Japan) was presumed to be among our number.

16 January 1942

From early in the morning I was on duty distributing drinking water. When I peered at the surface of the sea through a crack in the porthole cover, a ring of sunlight was reflected on the waves, and I marvelled at its beauty. After a miserable few days, today was fine. We all prayed for a safe voyage and for great happiness for our people in Japan. Then we noticed that two convoy vessels, each weighing about a thousand tons, were sailing in front of and behind our ship. One of the convoy vessels carried an aeroplane. Our ship was heading directly south.

All day the ship rolled badly. On top of that, the heat intensified. As a result, people fell sick one after another.

In the morning it rained intermittently. A roll call was taken.

We agreed that each group would take turns at drinking water duty. We requested the isolation of seriously ill patients who could be infectious and asked for some medication for those with high fever, but these requests were denied.

We used seawater for washing heavily soiled clothes. Consequently, the number of times we washed was reduced. There was no choice but to wear dirty clothes.

17 January 1942

The ship headed south over the ocean all day. We suddenly noticed that the two convoy vessels were no longer with us.

Today the water supply was cut off once. In the afternoon, the ship increased its speed. The sea became rough, and a strong wind blew in.

Thanks to this, inside the ship became cool. Our repeated request to separate women and children into a different room was rejected. We had to reorganise our groups. For the time being, we moved a family group who were in front of the toilet to another location, and we moved patients who suffered from diarrhoea to take their place.

18 January 1942
The sea was still rough today. In the afternoon, the ship rolled a lot.

We all found the tedium oppressive. Due to malnutrition everyone looked pale. Regarding our destination, most people were convinced that we were being taken to Australia.

19 January 1942
The sea was continually rough today. Mr Shōtarō Ueda from Lumajang died at ten thirty in the morning at the age of 63.

20 January 1942
Today the weather was rough again.

The body of Mr Ueda was buried at sea at ten thirty in the morning. We had a moment of silence for him.

21 January 1942
The sea was extremely rough today. We shivered as the coldness of the air gradually intensified. We wished we had at least a blanket.

22 January 1942
Lo Kok, who was Taiwanese, died at the age of 47. We repeatedly requested the army authority for treatment for sick people, but in vain.

23 January 1942
Although the cover of the delivery entrance had been off since 15 January, the cover was back on due to the cold weather. We felt revived. The temperature in the ship was rapidly going down as the ship headed south. People fell sick one after another, as we did not have enough warm clothes to protect us from the cold. It was regrettable that the patients

did not receive proper treatment. If we had received proper treatment, there would have been no casualties. Because we had lived in the land of perpetual summer for so long, we were not ready for such a sudden change of climate. However, we could not do anything but endure the current weather conditions. We all made a vow to look after ourselves even more carefully and to be ready for the day when we would be released. And then we prayed that the souls of the dead might rest in peace. It was nine thirty in the evening.

We had occasion to celebrate when a Taiwanese woman safely gave birth to a boy.

In the ship we had no access to luxury goods. Hence, if someone received a piece of cheap tobacco, several people smoked it in turn. On the other hand, there was an instance when one person secretly asked a soldier to buy him tobacco. The soldier pocketed most of the money and the person received only a small amount of tobacco. I sympathised with the predicament of those who smoked habitually.

However, we could not complain when we thought about the hardship experienced by our brave soldiers on the front line. Due to the lack of fruit and fresh vegetables, I felt something was going wrong in my body.

24 January 1942

It seemed as if the ship was heading in a south-easterly direction. The night before the ship pitched and rolled badly, and seawater came onto the deck over the gunwale, so we evacuated to the hold.

It was extremely cold at dawn.

25 January 1942

Of late I had felt that the morning coffee was cold, and the two tablespoons of green pea soup seemed like a feast. My appetite was poor due to seasickness.

Today at last a piece of meat was distributed together with some dried fish.

Because of the roll call, early in the morning we returned to the upper hatch from the lower hatch to which we had evacuated.

Suddenly, however, the roll call was suspended, and we had to return to the lower hatch. We did not know what was going on. We were perplexed. The soldiers, with drawn swords, went hither and thither not knowing what to do. Then the internees' numbered tags were handed down, first to our group, then to another group. My tag was number 59. It was almost noon by the time all internees received their number tags. We were quite surprised at their inept handling. When someone shouted that we would soon be landing, we were all delighted.

Night approached, and a rumour quickly spread that well over two hundred senior officials of the Dutch East Indies and their families were on board. I thought that it was reasonable for them to have boarded, as I remembered the rumour at the port in Cilacap about the governor general's escape to Australia.

We also heard that Singapore would fall within a week. We thought that the start of the Dutch East Indies campaign was approaching.

That night's dinner might have been our last supper, but the content was exactly the same as usual. They treated us like prisoners. Nevertheless, when I thought that we might be at the end of our miserable journey, I could not go to sleep for a long time. Even if we landed, our internment would continue, so there would be no change in our situation.

The fate of all human beings, let alone internees, is such that no one is guaranteed whether he will be alive tomorrow or not. As internees, we knew nothing of our fate. We had to endure any hardship and wait for the day of our release.

We should make our health our first priority and wait for the new day to arrive.

26 January 1942
We heard that we would be going ashore today. From early in the morning we began preparing for disembarkation. We just wrapped our clothes and

dishes, which were supplied during our Dutch East India internment, with the blanket which we spread on the floor for bedding.

Although we were anticipating landing, we could not see a single island.

After breakfast we were herded to the hold for the roll call. It took all morning to confirm our number tags.

In the afternoon, everyone was talking about where we would be interned after disembarking. Many rumours were flying around.

After dinner, we shared some sugar made from palm flowers. We do not know who obtained it.

We heard that we would be disembarking from the ship tomorrow. We chatted loudly and went to sleep at around ten o'clock.

27 January 1942

At around half past three in the morning, when I was marvelling at the surface of the sea, beautifully lit by the moon, an island with a lighthouse could be vaguely discerned on the port side. At around five o'clock, on the starboard side, an island emerged clearly. The ship was heading further to the east. We awaited our landing with great anticipation and began preparing for disembarkation.

At six o'clock, we were formally told that the ship would soon be landing. At around half past nine the ship entered a gulf, but we could not see a lot outside. Soon the land, and what appeared to be a town, emerged on the port side. Judging by the launches that were coming and going, the town must have been Adelaide. It was already noon when we were given our marching orders and told we were going to disembark. After lunch we were quarantined, then, for some reason, we were suddenly told that we would remain on board that night as well. It was fine all day, and we could at last see blue sky.

Today I volunteered to clean the toilet for the first time. Because every day I had been on duty taking turns at delivering drinking water, I had not had the opportunity to clean the toilet.

After dinner, the ship came alongside the pier. And then the Australian official in charge came to inspect our situation. He made a good impression on me, as his manner was very gentlemanly. He wore a smile all the time, as if he wished to show appreciation for the great pains we had taken.

It appeared that the pier guard was not strict. We felt that Australians were a part of the Great British nation.

28 January 1942

When the landing arrangements were made, the group leader reminded us that we should act prudently and quietly, and that we Japanese must not disgrace ourselves.

The group leader also told us that we should not stir up trouble with the arrogant Dutch East Indies soldiers who escorted us, and that we must restrain ourselves. Last night, an Australian officer came on to the ship guided by a Dutch East Indies soldier and looked around the hold. He asked whether we had been sick, and then he said to us, '*Sumimasen deshita* [We apologise for this.]' in fluent Japanese. We were particularly pleased to see the Australian officer unarmed. He had neither a gun nor a sword.

Unlike the Dutch East Indies soldiers, his manner was so gentle that we simply admired him. Incidentally, the Dutch East Indies officer was unarmed tonight. We thought that it was rather laughable.

Judging by this, we thought that the way the Australians treated us would be quite different from the way we had been treated. Hence, our first impressions were extremely good. The Australian officer was acting tactfully, like a British national, while he was with us.

We were disappointed to learn that we would spend another night on the ship.

Although it was cloudy in the morning, the weather was gradually clearing. We were able to see blue sky from the hatch. We spent all day exposing our whole body to the warm sunshine, thinking of a beautiful spring day in our Japanese homeland. From eight o'clock in the morning, an examination of any sick people was carried out, and the patients went ashore at about nine thirty to be sent to the hospital.

In the morning two female Australian volunteer soldiers came and inspected the ship.

29 January 1942
With disembarkation imminent, many people were busy washing clothes throughout the last night.

After breakfast, we were told to prepare for disembarkation and assembled expectantly. However, there had still been no order given to disembark even after noon. We waited impatiently for the order. It was already four thirty in the afternoon when we received the order to go ashore. It was arranged that we had dinner on the ship. After exchanging good-byes with the family groups who were to take a different route, we went to the pier in numerical order. We marched through the soldiers on guard and were herded on to a train. Surprisingly, almost all the soldiers were unarmed, and the train we went on consisted of second-class carriages. However, there were no carriages below second-class in Australia, so our carriages were the lowest ranked. We were still pleased to travel second-class this time, as in the Dutch East Indies we had to travel fourth-class, which was used only by the local people.

We split up and got on the train, 60 people per carriage, and were allowed to open the windows as soon as the train departed. The Australian soldiers' manner was extremely efficient, and their tolerant treatment pleased us. Soon after departure we received a blanket each, and we could protect ourselves from the cool temperature at night. The train departed at around six o'clock in the evening and was heading to Adelaide. I noticed comparatively low-set houses, which looked like *bunkajūtaku*,[4] here and there along the railway line. These houses were built of red bricks with a chimney protruding prominently. Perhaps these houses were built for the

4 A 'new style' Japanese house, characterised by the adoption of Western elements.

cool weather. And then I saw a wide expanse of grass fields, which were scorched due to the dry season. The grassland dotted with red brick houses looked like a scene in an oil painting. In addition, cows and horses were tranquilly grazing on stock farms. It was a picture of peace.

From time to time I saw a one-horse carriage driven by a rider with a fellow passenger, or an old-style car. It reminded me of the Britishness that values old-fashioned things.

We were approaching Adelaide. We passed through a district where many factories were built closely together, and then a uniquely Australian stock farm was seen. When I saw fat cows and horses ambling calmly amongst bushes looking for grass, I envied them. In the backyards of the houses seen along the railway line, apple trees, grape vines and orange trees bore fruit. It reminded me of my hometown.

When the train entered hilly areas, we greatly enjoyed the beautiful scenery of the sun setting on the horizon, a sunset such as can only be seen on the Australian continent.

By this time, the soldiers who had been escorting us had relaxed, and they began humming. They also gave us some tobacco and bread. Thanks to them, at last we could relax, as if we were going on a school excursion.

At night, the train gathered speed. It was still quite bright in the evening. It was still faintly light even after half past nine. (Of course, there was a time difference between Australia and the Dutch East Indies). Finally, the darkness of night fell, and the moon started shining brightly. We went to sleep without noticing it, but occasionally the sound of the train woke us up.

30 January 1942

The following day, 30 January, at around five o'clock in the morning, when I fully woke up, the train was speeding through grassland. Soon the train entered an area that looked like an orchard. We had been longing for some fruit for some time and wished we could eat some fresh fruit as soon as possible.

We were informed that we were getting off at six o'clock. We pictured in our mind the new camp, which we had not yet seen, and somehow, our spirits lifted. We thought that the new camp must be much better than the one in Java, judging by the way the Australian soldiers had been treating us till now.

The scenery surrounding us, which was emerging from the dim light of dawn, was an endless vineyard with only a few houses. The place where the train stopped was also in the middle of a vineyard. Shivering from the cold air, wearing only summer clothes, we started marching, carrying the blanket that had been given to us on the train on our shoulders. At the head of the line rode an officer on horseback. Escorted on both sides by guards, we marched quietly along a road that ran through vineyards planted with seedless grapes.

Later I heard that this area had been cultivated by returned soldiers from the First World War, and that not many people remained here. With the outbreak of the current war, many people had been recruited into the army or to munitions factories, and it was not so easy to harvest the fully ripened fruit. We marched about four kilometres, and finally we arrived at the entrance to the new camp, which we had been impatiently anticipating. As we suffered from cold and hunger while we were marching, stragglers were sent to the horse-drawn carriage that followed us. This was the very first marching we had done on foot since we had been detained in December the previous year. As our line stretched for nearly two hundred metres, and we wore such shabby clothes, we must have looked a sorry sight.

The soldiers, on the other hand, were very merry. While they were walking, they plucked some grapes from a grapevine near the road and ate them. The cluster of grapes was about a metre long.

The entrance to the camp was surrounded by wire and looked like a cage. They led one group at a time into the entrance and checked the numbers of the internees. After that, the front gate was opened, and internees were led into the camp. This whole operation was done in an Australian way. They opened and shut the front and back gates and counted internees as if counting sheep. Inside the camp, a group from Darwin, who had arrived earlier, pitched a tent, and kindly prepared food for our breakfast to welcome us.

Thanks to them, we enjoyed a feast starting with coffee, tea, and bread, which we had not enjoyed for a long time. We ate our fill and felt revived. We recovered from the fatigue of our miserable journey and we felt secure. After breakfast we underwent a physical examination and a search. We took off our clothes and faced the officer in charge. Since we had not had a proper bath for more than a month, the army doctor must have been surprised at the odd smell coming from our bodies. When I was searched, my memoir of the Sumowono camp was found hidden in my socks. To my surprise, I was only asked, 'Are you a newspaper reporter?' and my memoir was not confiscated. After the examination, we had curry rice, pie, and bread for lunch, then we had a proper shower. We were able to wash off the dirt accumulated over such a long period. We felt clean and settled into our tents. It had been decided that each tent would be occupied by six people. First, we spread a rubber sheet on the ground, then we put a mattress on top. We finished making our bedding with four blankets. Although we were a little bit uncomfortable sleeping directly on the ground, we did not have to worry about rain coming into our tent, as it was the dry season. However, the lighting in the tent was just a kerosene lamp. We could not help feeling miserable in the camp, living in a tent in a field.

In the Dutch East Indies internees were regarded as prisoners, and they treated us like coolies. However, we were deeply impressed with the way the Australian army treated us, as they considered us to be people who had been entrusted to their care by the British army. The only drawback was that we had to live in a tent and not in a proper building. In the meeting between our representatives and the Australian army officers, an old First Lieutenant told us, 'We will not do anything to cause you pain. Please do not worry, as we have ordered the guard soldiers to strictly obey our military rules. Although Japan and England are at war, we have absolutely no hatred towards you personally.'

However, among ordinary Australian people there were quite a few who had ill feelings towards us. Yesterday, when we were on the train under army guard, I noticed that an old woman who saw us, shook her fist at us. I thought that her son might have been killed in a battle with Japanese forces, and that she hated us.

There were two mess halls. Each mess hall had fifty tables with ten seats each. Five hundred people could have a meal all at once. They served plenty of vegetables. I was so pleased to be able to eat bread and potatoes, which I had been dreaming of.

After finishing dinner, we spend the first night in the tent. I marvelled at the beautiful sunset. I almost forgot the passage of time when I saw the sun setting on the horizon of this magnificent and vast continent.

And then I hurried into the tent when the signal for lights-out was given at ten o'clock. The dim twilight continued for a long time, and kerosene lights began turning on one after another. Night was gradually falling on the tents that stood in a row. This camp was known as 14B camp. Japanese people sent from New Caledonia and Darwin had already been interned for more than a month. When our group joined them, the number of internees grew to 920.

Tents were pitched in 11 rows. In each row 16 tents were lined up. (One row remained unoccupied.) An hour after our arrival, about 510 people from Sumatra were interned in a neighbouring camp.

CHAPTER 5

LOVEDAY INTERNMENT CAMP DIARY. PART 1. FROM 31 JANUARY TO 15 AUGUST 1942

PROLOGUE

As I have already mentioned, Loveday camp, to which we were sent, was located on vacant land in an orchard cultivated by returned soldiers from the First World War. The place looked desolate, and irrigation pipes were buried everywhere. Camp 14[1] was set in this deserted area. A mess hall, a kitchen, a bathroom, a washroom, and a toilet were the only proper buildings. The places where we spent most of our time were not buildings but mere tents, which were put up everywhere in the camp.

At first, each tent was shared by six internees. As the number of internees grew, eight people were crammed into each tent. We were often annoyed by rain and wind. On rainy and windy days, we hardly slept all night. For our bed, we first covered a small area of ground with a rubber sheet and then spread straw. We had only four blankets for the cold nights. While the rain mercilessly wet our beds, the strong wind made our tents scream. Consequently, we had to work hard all the time not only to make drainage around the tent, but also to put stones on the edge of the tent to stop it flapping.

After the departure of the repatriated group, all the tents were finally removed, and all internees were ordered to move to huts on 27 August.

---

1 After Camps 9 and 10, Camp 14 was the third and final of the camps to be constructed at Loveday. It was divided into four compounds or sections: 14A held Italian prisoners, 14B and 14C held Japanese prisoners and 14D held mainly German and Italian prisoners.

Although each hut was constructed of timber, the roof was made of corrugated tin sheeting without any ceiling. On top of that, we had no proper walls, but only corrugated tin sheeting as cladding. Hence, our huts became like a fridge in winter, and a sauna in summer. Once the hot wind attacked, we shut all the windows, sprinkled cold water on the floor, covered our faces with wet towels and lay down. Then we waited until the hot wind died down. This was the only way to cope with the hot wind. The strong wind mercilessly blew sand into the hut and we all felt miserable. We were internees who did not know when our term would end. We were all shaken. I could not help wishing we had a proper ceiling and walls to protect us from the heat and the cold, like the huts made for the soldiers.

Next, I shall talk about the food supply. The food distributed in the camp was for the most part the same as that for the army. However, I could not help doubting its quality. (Perhaps, from the quantity point of view, there was no difference between them.) Australia played a role in the logistics of the Allied Powers and supplied food for various countries, starting with England. It would have been a priority for Australia to supply food for its own people and it must have been difficult to supply food for the internees. Considering the terrible food shortages at the end of the war in Japan, which I learnt about after returning home, the internees in Australia were much more fortunate than the Japanese people who suffered from food shortages in Japan. However, an Australian brigadier who visited the camp after the war ended gave orders to reduce the quantity of food for internees, as the Japanese army's treatment of the Australian prisoners of war in Singapore was not satisfactory.

As for medical treatment, it was decided that from now on dental treatment and treatment for the patients who suffered from minor illness should be suspended. However, I heard that the number of prisoners of war at the time of the fall of Singapore was about one hundred and fifty thousand, and presumably a lot of things went wrong. Thus, it would have been extremely difficult for the Japanese army to obtain enough food and medicine. I also understand how frustrating it was for the enemy side to learn of the treatment of their prisoners of war. However, because the war had already ended, I wished they would have continued at least the medical supplies.

Let us talk about labour issues.

While prisoners of war were forced to work for payment, civilian internees were not forced to work. Consequently, no payment was made. There was no other way to obtain income than to engage in work outside the camp (daily wages one shilling).

At the beginning of our internment, we refused to engage in work outside the camp as it only benefitted the enemy. Because some internees wished to engage in work outside of the camp in order to have some pocket money, the Japanese as a group accepted the demand of the army with the condition that the work should be light.

I remember that the available work included growing vegetables, growing poppies or rubber, and looking after pigs. Work of a special nature was also available.

However, those who engaged in such work could not erase the thought that they were assisting the enemy. Because the poppies were used to produce morphine as an anaesthetic, internees tried to grow poppies without any flowers. They also tried to inhibit the growth of young rubber plants. As a result of their efforts, almost all the plants died, and their work was in vain. Those who worked for the pig farm took some piglets to the group and ate them.

The following notes are not a diary in the full sense, but rather daily memos.

31 January 1942
After spending the first night in a tent in Australia, we all admired the view of floating clouds reflecting the light of the rising sun. We almost

forgot the time and kept looking at the scenery with our bodies shivering from the cold dawn air. It was scenery such as can only be seen on the Australian continent.

After the breakfast, head-and-shoulder photos were taken of us, and fingerprints were taken for the purpose of exchanging a list of names, in accordance with the agreement between Japan and England regarding prisoners of war. Because I had not had a chance to have a haircut since I had been captured, my hair and beard had grown unrestrained. On top of that, the photo was taken not with a prison number but with an identification tag that was hanging from my neck. I thought that even if my family living in Japan had the opportunity to see my photo, they would not have recognised me.

When we returned to the tent, we started gathering stones which were used to stop the tent flapping in the wind. Incidentally, the commanding officer of the camp (a captain) told us not to worry, as internees would be treated according to a mutual agreement between Japan and England. Then the camp leadership was negotiated. Its structure was as follows. Under the committee that negotiated with the army, a 'street leader' was elected for each row of tents, and a group leader was elected for every four tents.

In addition, this morning an information bureau was organised, and the first newspaper news was released. According to the news, our army had begun the Dutch East Indies campaign, a big military unit had been sent for the Singapore campaign from Hainan Island, and the Allied Powers had offered assistance to the American army, etc ... In the afternoon, the temperature suddenly went up, and it became very hot and humid. There was a huge difference between the temperature in the morning and evening and that during the daytime. I was surprised at the continental weather, to which I was not yet accustomed. Moreover, the place I was sent to was close to the desert. Every time I saw a thick cloud of dust arising, I started worrying about my future in the camp.

Loveday 14 B Camp Hut Plan

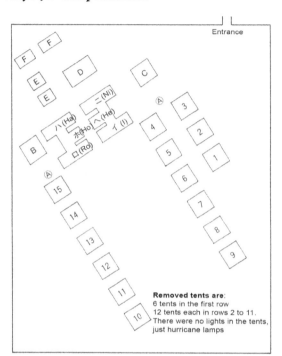

A. Huts (barracks) are numbered
   1–15 (36 feet x 63 feet)
   I, Ro, Ha, Ni – mess halls
   (24 x 108 ft)
   Ho, He – kitchens (24 x 68 ft)
B. Medical facility (15 x 24 ft)
C. Office (24 x 60 ft)
D. Bathroom and Laundry
   (30 x 108 ft)
E. Washrooms with basins
   (14 x 42 ft)
F. Toilets (12 x 60 ft)
   Perimeter 3,610 feet (1091 m)
   Area 20,520 tubo
   (67,839 sq. m)

Each soldier dressed differently. Some wore shorts, and others wore long trousers. Just by looking at them, we knew how striking the difference in temperature was. We did our washing, which we had not done for a long time. Mr Togami was elected as a group leader.

1 February 1942

The rising sun shone through clouds scattered across the blue sky. What a beautiful dawn it was! It was unusually warm in the morning. The temperature rose quickly, and by noon it became so hot that it reminded me of summer in mainland Japan. We were absorbed in conversation in our tent all day. Unlike the outside world, we had no job to engage us. We had nothing to do but kill time. The sun was still shining at seven o'clock in the evening. When the sun was setting in the west, a big round moon rose on the horizon. By that time, the temperature had dropped, and it became cool. We cheerfully set off to the laundry to do our washing.

The soil we were standing on was quite sandy, reminiscent of the sandy coast where we used to go swimming.

The internment camp was surrounded by coils of barbed wire and floodlights were positioned at several points. The internees were prohibited from approaching the barbed wire. We were warned that if we came too close to the barbed wire, a guard in the lookout post would relentlessly fire the machine gun. We were detained in a cage with a circumference of about a kilometre, surrounded by barbed wire, like monkeys in a zoo. How many months and years, I wondered, would we spend in this camp with little hope of release?

Far from our homeland, we had to live in a foreign country in the southern hemisphere. Moreover, we had to live the dreary life of an all-male group, despite having all spent our lives differently before internment. Everyone was the head of a household, and we were a thousand in total. This number was equivalent to that of the whole population of a small village. It would be extremely difficult for the leaders to manage life in the camp.

There was no hierarchy in the camp, and everything, starting with clothes and food, was equal. We could not hope to satisfy individual desires. I thought that it was important to get used to communal life, and that it would be a good opportunity to learn that which I had not previously had a chance to learn. I sincerely wished to raise the level of my culture.

It was time for lights out, and the light in the tent was turned off. However, the moonlight was so bright that I could not go to sleep. I could not help thinking of my home country, and I sincerely wished that I would be free to go home soon. The night was deepening so quietly and peacefully that no one could imagine that a war was going on outside.

2 February 1942

I rose at six o'clock, and again witnessed a beautiful sunrise. It was a beautiful morning on that vast plain, where I could not see any hill, let alone a mountain. It was the most refreshing time of the day.

Every time I saw several heavy smokers buy some tobacco with money they borrowed from people who had arrived in the camp earlier, and share the same cigarette in turn, I could not help feeling sorry for them. The camp rules were formally announced. They stipulated the following routine:

6:30	rise
7:20	roll call in the mess hall
7:30	breakfast, cleaning outside and inside tents by 9 o'clock
9:30	assemble in lines in front of tents for inspection by the commanding officer.
	(Sick people to be examined from 9 o'clock.)
12:30	lunch
5:30	roll call in front of the mess hall (checking the number of internees)
5:40	dinner
9:30	prepare for lights out
10:00	lights out.

In addition, it was prohibited for more than three people to leave their tent from lights out to the time of rising, even to go to the toilet. The toilets were located in two buildings that were some distance from the tents.

We were ordered to select ten people from our row who wished to do paid work. They would be engaged mainly in cleaning. Payment would be one shilling per day. Today water taps for irrigation were all turned on at once, and we were allowed to use them to grow vegetables. Those interested started sowing vegetable seeds.

As it was the dry season, the grasses in the plain were all dead. But in the shadow of the tent, some weeds began sprouting. Mr Togami took up his position as street leader.

3 February 1942

This morning the commanding officer inspected our camp for the first time. We were informed of camp matters that required attention. It was another fine day. It became hot and humid around noon. Then a strong wind raised a thick cloud of dust. All group members stayed in the tent all day and rested. In the evening, the Southern Cross could be seen very clearly in the sky. Then a big moon, just like a painting, appeared on the horizon, and consoled us all.

4 February 1942

We had another fine day, and every day was much the same. Mr Andō from Dōmei News Agency,[2] who had taken up the position of compound leader, resigned, as he had incurred the displeasure of the army authorities. We heard that he tried to push forward strong measures.

It turned out that the total number of tents was 168 and the total number of internees was 913.

In the evening, a musical concert of recorded music was held, and reminded us of our dear country. We wished for strenuous effort on the home front to back up the armed forces.

Matters upon which we agreed today:

One person per group should be elected for dishwashing duty. Ten people per row should take turns setting the tables. Twenty-four people per row should be on duty for chores such as cleaning basins and bathrooms. They should work on a day shift.

Tobacco arrived at the canteen. However, nobody in our group had money to buy tobacco. There was no choice but to share any tobacco that they were given. In the end, one person became so desperate to smoke that

---

2   Dōmei News Agency was the official news agency of the Empire of Japan.

for tobacco he substituted dead grass wrapped in toilet paper. There was another person who substituted tea leaves wrapped in paper. I sympathised with heavy smokers.

5 February 1942

Thanks to the kindness of a charitable man, I finally had a haircut after eighty days. Of course, it was done free of charge. He borrowed hair clippers from the group from Darwin.

Today Mr Sakimura from the Yokohama Specie Bank became compound leader. We obtained some articles from *The Advertiser* newspaper dated 21 January from the army authority. According to them, N. Y. AAP [3] reported that Prime Minister Tōjō, Minister for Foreign Affairs Tōgō, and Minister of the Navy Shimada, each made a congressional speech. The Minister for Foreign Affairs made it clear that Japan would faithfully adhere to the Soviet-Japan Neutrality Pact. The Minister of the Navy reported on military gains in Manila and Hawaii, and the Japanese Army landed on Manado on 1 January, etc.

Today we requested underwear, a toothbrush, a hairbrush, and a second-hand set of clothing to be distributed.

Paid working positions were advertised, such as cleaning the stable, tree felling, making fences. Seventy-seven people applied for a job. Every day two people from each tent should be on toilet cleaning duty in turn.

We had peaches for dinner ... Finally, we had some fruit to eat.

6 February 1942

It suddenly became popular in each tent to make a shrubbery surrounded by small stones. Today I felt that it was even more hot and humid than it was in Java. What was more, our tent was shaken badly by a whirlwind.

There was news that a strong Japanese military unit had landed at an army base in the foreign occupied territory of the Dutch East Indies.

---

3   The New York bureau of Australian Associated Press.

7 February 1942

It was unusually cloudy this morning. The sky was so dark that it reminded me of a snowy day in mainland Japan. After our morning inspection, we cut down weeds, and put them under our rubber sheets. Then we put small stones along the edges of the tent, so that we could avoid wind damage. From ten o'clock on, the weather improved, but then it became hot again.

Today's news.

While our army fought in Johor on 3 February, the Japanese Air force performed splendidly.

Tokyo radio reported that the British Army escaped from Singapore on twenty-five ships.

It also reported that our Japanese Army began their assault on Java. At the same time, the Dutch East Indies government acknowledged that northern Borneo was occupied by the Japanese Army on 24 January. A.P.[4] reported on 6 February: 'The Japanese Army sailed through the Johor Strait and launched an all-out attack on Singapore on 5 February.'

I also heard that English and Russian women and children who were evacuated to Australia lived in tents as well.

9 February 1942

This morning it was cloudy again. Recently the weather has been rather unsettled. As the wind changes direction several times a day, the temperature goes up and down rapidly. Today fifty-one people were hospitalised with fevers. I also had a slight cold.

10 February 1942

People fell sick with fever one after another.

Vaccination. We were vaccinated against typhoid fever.

11 February 1942

Today was Empire Day. With the permission of the army authorities, we

---

4 Associated Press.

worshipped His Imperial Palace from afar at seven o'clock in the morning. We prayed for the Imperial Army's soldiers' continued good fortune in the war. Following that, the Japanese national anthem *Kimigayo* [thy glorious reign] was sung and a ceremony was held. Regrettably, however, I could not participate, due to a high fever. As my fever rose to over 39 degrees, I was hospitalised at four o'clock in the afternoon. I was examined by a German doctor. I learned that one hundred and three people, including Mr Imagawa, had been brought to the neighbouring internment camp.

12 February 1942
Yesterday I was hospitalised due to my high fever. As my fever went down, I was discharged. Unlike the tent, the hospital had double ceilings and was surrounded by heat resistant walls. I was comfortable in the hospital as I could avoid the heat. However, the food was just deplorable. At around four o'clock in the afternoon, when the rain stopped, I returned to the tent carrying my blanket and straw mattress on my back. After dinner I received one shilling worth of military currency from Mr Sakimura, and I bought ten pieces of washing soap. We divided them into three and shared them. I spoked to Mr Imagawa over the fence. While I was in hospital, I was ordered to become a member of the general affairs section for the group. I attended a whole committee meeting.

Today a set of clothes was distributed (these were second-hand military uniforms dyed red). The canteen will be open from eleven till twelve in the morning, and from seven till eight in the evening.

13 February 1942
We had a lovely morning today. I was on dishwashing duty. I helped to fill in disembarkation cards all day.

14 February 1942
I was on dishwashing duty. I helped to fill in disembarkation cards today as well.

News: Lieutenant General Yamashita issued an ultimatum to the English commander defending Singapore.

15 February 1942
News: The Japanese Army bombed and sank ten of the twenty-five troop ships in a convoy carrying British soldiers retreating from Singapore. The Japanese Army occupied the main fortresses in Singapore on 13 February.

One journalist reported that the military force of the Japanese Army included one hundred and fifty thousand Philippine soldiers, one hundred and twenty thousand Malaysian soldiers, seventy-five thousand Dutch East Indies soldiers, seventy-five thousand Burmese soldiers and thirty thousand reservists.[5]

16 February 1942
We had a dental examination.

17 February 1942
News: A cease-fire was declared in Singapore at ten o'clock in the evening on 15 February. A British delegation consisting of four people arrived at the Japanese headquarters with a white flag at around half past two in the afternoon. They formally surrendered. They left at a quarter past four in the afternoon.

According to a Tokyo broadcast, they signed a cease-fire agreement at around seven o'clock in the evening. Then the cease-fire was announced at 10 o'clock in the evening. The reason for the surrender was the destruction of the reservoir by the Japanese Army. On the Dutch East Indies front an assault was launched against Sumatra. The Japanese Army began an all-out attack on the eastern coast of Sumatra on 15 February. Batavia

---

5 It is not clear what source Koike is drawing on here. At this time the internees were permitted to receive uncensored newspapers, but from April 1942 newspapers entering the compounds were subjected to censorship. When the course of the war turned in the Allies' favour, censorship was relaxed and eventually abolished. It is conceivable – but unproven – that the internees had managed to set up a radio receiver.

radio reported that the Japanese Army was advancing towards Palembang. The Dutch East Indies resorted to a scorched earth policy and gave orders to destroy major facilities.

17 February 1942

News: Before launching an assault from the sea, the Japanese Army parachuted several hundred troops into an area near Palembang. They headed for the oil refinery.

18 February 1942

It rained with thunder and lightning before dawn. Thanks to the rain, the dust storm eased. The roll call was suspended. Among our group there are some who are good with their hands. Some people made scissors and knives using an old oil drum. Others even made *geta* [Japanese wooden clogs] and pipes using eucalyptus firewood. It has been decided that from now on we will gather at half past eight and worship His Imperial Palace from afar and then do radio calisthenics.

News: Dōmei News Agency: The Japanese Army entered the fortress in Singapore at eight o'clock in the morning on 16 February, with many tanks. Our fleet entered the port on 15 February.

General Percival[6] reported to the Allied supreme commander in South East Asia, General Wavell, on 15 February as follows: 'There was no choice but to surrender, as we lacked water, ammunition, and food. We held out to the last and continued to fight, but women, children and the wounded were withdrawn. The remaining forces numbered fifty-five thousand.'

Tokyo radio: The Japanese Army authorities allowed one thousand English soldiers to arm to keep the peace in Singapore. Lieutenant General Yamashita[7] promised to ensure the safety of women and children.

---

6 Lieutenant-General Arthur Percival commanded British Commonwealth forces during the Japanese Malayan Campaign and the subsequent Battle of Singapore. He was captured and held as a POW in Changi.
7 Tomoyuki Yamashita led Japanese forces during the invasion of Malaya and the Battle of Singapore.

Batavia radio reported: 'On 6 February Palembang was occupied. However, we destroyed the oil field. A strong Japanese sea convoy was located in the Bangka Strait. An attack on this territory is imminent.'

19 February 1942
Cloudy. It was cool, thanks to a strong southerly wind.

At two o'clock in the afternoon we left for Barmera Station to receive the baggage we brought on the *Cremer*. We travelled by truck on the bumpy road to Barmera. I saw fields of grapes, peaches, mandarins and pumpkins on both sides of the road. Perhaps because this was a newly cultivated area, several unplanted fields could be seen. I could not get a full view of the town, as the truck had a cover, but it seemed to be fairly small.

I noticed that there was a post office, a theatre and a bar.

This town may be a place where soldiers can get some rest and recreation.

The station seemed to be a hastily built military stop. The building itself was splendid, but not many facilities were to be found. Soon the truck pulled up beside the train, and the baggage was transferred. The baggage was substantially damaged. Among it there was one trunk with a broken lock and missing contents .... The baggage was brought back to the camp and temporarily stored in the army warehouse.

I was quite excited, as I had not been out of the camp for a long time. I was looking forward to seeing the outside world. When the truck was about to enter the town of Barmera, a lake could be seen to the north.

On the way back to the camp, I saw a whole family picking grapes. I could not help shouting with admiration when I saw a young woman with strong arms briskly riding a horse.

19 February 1942
News: On 19 February, a Japanese combat plane appeared over Sydney. It

appeared that the plane had flown from a submarine. In the evening the Japanese plane returned eastwards to the coast.

(Tokyo radio) In Singapore a few people were still resisting. The Japanese Army had occupied the English navy base and other areas. Governor Thomas and his wife[8] were captured by our army. Japan renamed Singapore as Shōnan. Our Army bombed Batavia and Palembang. A military unit parachuted into Palembang had achieved the desired results by 9 o'clock in the morning and secured the oil refinery.

A Japanese sea convoy arrived at the mouth of the Musi River. The Dutch East Indies resorted to a scorched earth policy. They set a fire to an oil tank. The burning oil flowed to the coast. The mouth of the Musi River turned into a raging inferno. Palembang radio fell silent.

Philippines front line: Our Army commanded by Lieutenant General Honma fought fiercely on Batan Island.

20 February 1942
Cloudy. I visited the headquarters as a carpentry assistant. I went there by truck. I had not been outside the camp for a while. Of course, my sole purpose was sightseeing. Recruitment for wood cutting began.

21 February 1942
I rose at five o'clock. I was on duty setting up the tables. After breakfast, we cleaned the mess hall. I peeled potatoes and pumpkins. I was ashamed of my clumsiness with my hands.

After a cloudy morning it became fine. A youth baseball game was held (the second-generation team won). Wood cutting applications now exceed one hundred. The baggage which we had been putting in order was returned to its owners. Those who received the baggage were almost all residents of the so-called *gairyō* [that is, all the Dutch East Indies islands except for Java], and medicines were all confiscated. Recently robberies have

---

8 Sir Shenton Thomas was the last Governor of the Straits Settlements. After his capture he spent the remainder of the war in Changi Prison.

occurred one after another. We decided to tighten our guarding of each row. In the evening, an amateur entertainment show by internees was held.

Amateur entertainment show by internees

The show began with a funny introduction by Mr Okamura. We forgot that we were internees and became high-spirited. Representatives from each row gave enthusiastic performances such as mimicry, *naniwa-bushi* [recitation and singing of stories of loyalty and human feeling with samisen accompaniment], whistling, choral singing, *seitai-mosha* [imitation of a person's voice], *ōryokukō-bushi* [a popular song during the Taisho era, which began with raft men who come to the Yalu River on the border between North Korea and China to find work], *yasuki-bushi* [originally sung as entertainment for boatmen from seaports on the Japan Sea during the latter part of Edo era], etc. Everyone did very well for amateurs, with appealing performances. At the end, Mr Amano from Nan'yō Kaiun [Nan'yō Shipping] delivered a comic monologue. His story was so funny that we were all in convulsions. This was the first recreation we had had in a long time. At nine o'clock in the evening the show ended. We had to fit the remaining program into our next show.

News: General Count Terauchi, commander of the Southern Expeditionary Army Group, bombed Darwin twice on 19 February. In the Philippines, waves of Japanese soldiers landed one after another. In Singapore, a hundred and ten thousand people, including Indians, were captured by the Japanese Army.

22 February 1942

News: Tokyo radio

Both Lieutenant-General Percival and Major General Bennett[9] (a commander of the Australian Air Force) were confined in Changi fortress.

---

9   Major Gordon Bennett, commander of the 8th Australian Division, controversially managed to escape from Singapore before its fall, while his men became prisoners of the Imperial Japanese Army.

23 February 1942
Fine.

A strong wind blew in the morning, and we had poor visibility due to a thick cloud of dust. Sometimes small stones were flying through the air.

24 February 1942
Fine. A staff member from the Swiss consulate came to the camp.[10]

The content of his talk was as follows:

Some issues had arisen regarding a ship for the exchange of internees. The Japanese side wanted the repatriation of all internees. (The other party wished to prioritise sick people, women, and children.)

In regard to food, we requested an increase in the quantity of rice from the army authorities.

We requested the distribution of as many clothes as were distributed to C Camp.

In regard to medical treatment, we requested a complete set of equipment for dental surgery. We also requested some false teeth.

Spectacles ... we requested more eye-examinations.

For reference, at present the number of Japanese internees is as follows.

Tatura (for family groups)	870
Hay	900
Loveday C Compound	540
Loveday B Compound	740
Wood Cutting Camp	150
Total	3200

Everyone helped prepare an individual card for dental examinations. For the first time we had no bread at lunch. Safety razors, towels and toothpaste were distributed. From 6 o'clock in the evening we had a baseball game between rows.

---

10 As the designated 'Protecting Power', Switzerland was entitled to send representatives to check on the conditions of Japanese and other internees in internment camps such as Loveday.

The first supply of clothing.
Cartoon by Mr Ishikane.

The following is a short description of the baseball games.

Players entered the field behind a pennant. We worshipped His Imperial Palace from afar. Then we observed a minute's silence for the spirits of dead soldiers to show our gratitude. Following an opening ceremony for the baseball games, in which our compound leader pitched the first ball, the first game began: the group from Borneo played against the group from Batavia. Cheering for one's own team was heated. The Batavia group won with a score of 8A–7. As the balls and bats were made hurriedly, the game progressed rather unfairly. Nonetheless, all played in a sportsmanlike way. We fully enjoyed the game and it ended happily.

25 February 1942

A clear sky. It was hot. A tent inspection was carried out. I had a haircut for the second time since I entered the camp. For dinner we had some mandarins. It was rare for us to have a mandarin. I last ate them in Surabaya. Recently the amount of bread distributed has been decreasing.

We had a baseball game: the group from Batavia played against the group from Borneo. The Batavia group won the game with a score of 4–3.

News: N.Y. on 23 February, the American Army was quiet on all fronts in Luzon.

N.Y. on 25 February, from Los Angeles an attack by a Japanese combat plane was reported as follows: 'A blackout was ordered in the neighbouring area at three o'clock in the morning on 25 February. Then anti-aircraft guns were fired for thirty minutes. It appeared that the enemy plane had flown either from a small aircraft carrier or from a submarine.'

26 February 1942

Cloudy. It was a little cooler. It was decided that a wood cutting group consisting of one hundred and eleven people will depart on 1 March. Consequently, an amateur entertainment show was held in the evening to farewell them. The compound leader made a speech. Mr Yoshiyama made a speech to express the group's gratitude. I received a telegram [in English] sent from mainland Japan on the twelfth of February via Geneva: 'All fine here. Endeavour. Fumiko.'[11]

We had a baseball game. The group from Semarang played against the allied group from Darwin and New Caledonia. The former won the game with a score of 5-4.

A former famous player amused us with his unskilful demonstration, as he was playing baseball for the first time in ten years. We used a cudgel instead of a bat and a small stone wrapped in rags as a ball.

Today I helped to distribute old shoes.

27 February 1942
A clear sky. It was hot. Recently some people began complaining about our dreary life in the camp. We have to conserve goods. We are persistently asked to collect empty cans. The following was printed on a paper tobacco box: 'Avoid waste. Save this box for further use.'

27 February 1942
We were told that there will be one hundred and four new arrivals at the camp tomorrow. We were busy putting up tents.

28 February 1942
At around two o'clock in the afternoon one hundred and two old people from New Caledonia arrived at the camp. We had a baseball game. Two groups from Surabaya played against each other. The group from the ninth row won the game with a score of 5-3.

At night we gave a farewell party for the wood cutting group. We celebrated their departure with a band playing. Mr Higawa gave an address. Mr Nakamura made a speech to encourage the group.

News: Judging from the bombing of Semarang by Japanese combat planes, a landing on Semarang by the Imperial Army is imminent.

---

11 Fumiko was Koike's wife.

1 March 1942

A clear sky. At nine o'clock in the morning an advance party for the wood cutting wood group departed. At one o'clock in the afternoon the party divided into groups and set out in six trucks. Then two cars filled with goods followed.

I was on duty doing chores. A strong north wind blew. To make matters worse, the sun shone harshly. Our hut became so humid that we felt like we were in hell.

We had a baseball game. This time two groups from Batavia played against each other. The first team won with a score of 9A-8. At night, a big moon could be seen in the middle of the sky. It reminded us of the harvest moon in mainland Japan. We heard a band cheerfully playing in the Italian camp. From our camp we called for an encore many times. Japanese and Italian internees fraternised peacefully. We seemed to console each other for being poor internees.

2 March 1942

A clear sky. Although it was a little hot, it was getting easier to stand the heat in the morning and in the evening. I was on duty doing chores.

Today for breakfast we had eggs, which we had not eaten for a long time.

We had a baseball game. The Semarang group from the ninth row played against the group from Surabaya. The Surabaya group won one-sidedly with a score of 8-0. We admired the full moon again tonight. We have heard a band playing in the Italian camp for two nights in a row.

3 March 1942

Today we had a slice of rockmelon each.

From early in the morning a hot wind blew mercilessly into our tent, and occasionally a whirlwind passed. The tent became like a blazing inferno. For dinner we had some sponge cake.

News: On 28 February Bandung radio reported that the Japanese Army had landed at Bantam, Indramayu and Lembang.[12] On 27 February a major naval battle was fought in the Java Sea. [The allies] found forty Japanese sea vessels heading for east Java, escorted by a twenty strong fleet, which they attacked. Both sides suffered serious losses.[13]

4 March 1942
Cloudy.

I left my tent at half past five, as I was on meal preparation duty. Today a hot wind again stirred up the dust. A baseball game was played. Group A from Batavia played against the Surabaya group from the ninth row. The game was won by the Surabaya group 6:4. Tonight I went to sleep without a blanket for the first time. According to a newspaper which we obtained today, the Red Cross is trying to supply food for the Japanese prisoners of war detained in Australia.[14] Everyone was pleased to hear that.

5 March 1942
A strong wind blew all day. I was on dishwashing duty. Mr Zai died. I felt cold at night.

News: On 3 March the Dutch East Indies abandoned Batavia and moved their government to Bandung.

6 March 1942
A clear sky. At half past four in the morning I observed a minute of silence for the spirit of Mr Zai.

News: An American broadcast reported that the Japanese Army was advancing on all fronts in Java.

7 March 1942
Fine. In the morning it became chilly. From seven o'clock in the evening

---

12 This reference gives further weight to the idea that the internees might have had access to a radio receiver.
13 In fact, the Allied losses in the Battle of the Java Sea were much greater than the Japanese losses.
14 The Japanese POWs were held at a POW camp in Cowra, New South Wales.

an amateur entertainment show was held for the second time. It included mimicry, *nagauta* [a long epic song with samisen accompaniment developed in Edo in the early 17th century], *naniwa-bushi* [a type of narrative ballad chanted by a reciter to a samisen accompaniment], *manzai* [a two-person comedy act], *mandan* [a comic monologue], and *yoneyama-jinku* [a lively Yoneyama folk song]. It finished at half past nine in the evening.

On 4 March UP[15] (New York) reported that Japan was in command of the sea. They acknowledged the superiority of the Japanese Air Force.

8 March 1942

Fine. We received the following report written on 6 March from the wood cutting group: 'Our work began on 3 March.'

For dinner we had grapes.

News: According to a report from London, Japan has occupied Batavia. Moreover, the Japanese Army has advanced within twenty-five kilometres of Bandung, and within forty kilometres of Surabaya.

In Sydney, the first air-raid alarm sounded.

9 March 1942

Fine. It was cool. After breakfast we had an opening ceremony for the *sumō* wrestling ring.

Tokyo radio reported that the Japanese Army entered the Batavia fortress without bloodshed.

10 March 1942

We worshipped His Imperial Palace from afar as today was Army Commemoration Day. We showed our gratitude to the Imperial Army soldiers and observed a minute of silence for the spirits of heroic fallen soldiers. We all cheered up as the Java campaign was nearing an end.

We requested permission to subscribe to a newspaper. I was given some toothpaste from Mr Sakimura. We had a baseball game. This time a group

---

15 United Press.

We don't have to pay anything for all this.
Cartoon by Mr Okamura.

from the Kansai region played against those who came from the Kantō region. The Kantō group won with a score of 9–1.

A trophy made from empty cans was given to the winning team. (We divided people into two groups by separating them with reference to the city of Hikone in Shiga prefecture.)

Mr Tōsaku Nagao died.

News: The Japanese Army landed at Lae in New Guinea. Moresby was bombed.

11 March 1942

Cloudy. At eleven o'clock in the morning we observed a minute of silence for the spirit of Mr Nagao.

We had grapes for lunch. Today the distribution of bread was delayed, so we baked some cake.

News: Tokyo radio reported that at nine o'clock on the morning of 9 March the Dutch East Indies Air Force had agreed to surrender unconditionally. Ninety-three thousand Dutch East Indies soldiers and five thousand European soldiers surrendered.

Van Mook[16] arrived in Adelaide on 9 March. The Japanese Army occupied Salamaua on 8 March.

12 March 1942

Cloudy. It was hot and humid. A strong southerly wind blew. We had eggs for breakfast. We had no butter for lunch. We had grapes (we have had fruit four times so far.)

13 March 1942

Fine. At around six o'clock in the afternoon forty-seven people were transferred by truck to this camp from the Hay Camp. Everyone was advanced in age. Five people among them were immediately hospitalised, and others who were healthy went to their tents at eight o'clock.

---

16 Hubertus van Mook, a Dutch administrator in the East Indies.

14 March 1942

Talking to the people from the Hay Camp, our conversation grew lively. It was fine and a bit cold. At night, a waxing crescent moon could be seen in the sky, and we felt colder. Outside our camp the movement of trucks became frequent. At around ten o'clock in the evening I heard a train whistle. I felt as if war clouds were drifting even to Australia.

An inspector came from the Adelaide headquarters.

I was on meal preparation duty. I cleaned the floor of the mess hall. I had great difficulty peeling potatoes and carrots.

16 March 1942

Fine. A tent inspection was carried out. It was hot and humid in the afternoon. I helped people on duty doing chores.

We opened a Japanese language course.

Thanks to Mr Yūzaburō Tanaka, a Japanese language class for Taiwanese people had previously been conducted three times a week. Eight people had participated in that class. Because of the enthusiasm shown by the participants, the Japanese group decided to start a proper Japanese language course. It finally started on 16 March. About seventy people aged between fifteen and sixty expressed interest.

One class is at a *Jinjō* [17] grade three or four level with Mr Oda in charge. Six people are enrolled.

Another class with Mr Lee and another person in charge. The enrolment is twenty-five.

Another class at grade one level with Mr Yūzaburo Tanaka and others in charge. Thirty-three people are enrolled.

17 March 1942

Fine. From evening a strong southerly wind blew. It grew cold.

News: According to [a report from] N.Y. on 15 March, the Japanese

---

17 *Jinjō* is the name given to the elementary school system that operated in Japan from 1886 to 1941.

Army landed on the northern coast of Sumatra and entered the fortress in Medan without bloodshed.

18 March 1942

Fine. It was a bit warmer. The preliminary round of a *shōgi*[18] tournament was held. We began practising *sumō* wrestling.

Lately the sunrise has been at around half past six. We had grapes for dinner. When the rollcall was carried out in the evening, we were told that the number of the people per tent was to increase to eight from now on. Consequently, lights out was extended for thirty minutes to allow groups to reorganise. It has been decided that the following eight people are to be allocated to our tent. We decided to name our tent the 'eight best people's house'. The members of our tent are:

    The Yokohama Specie Bank ... Togami, Fujii and Koike (three people)
    Nan'yō Kaiun [Nan'yo Shipping] ... Itonaga and Mikumo (two people)
    The Taiwan Bank ... Oda
    Tōyō Menka [Orient Cotton] ... Nagai (Y.)
    Nihon Menka [Japan Cotton] ... Yoneda

19 March 1942

Fine. Lately the sun rises at around seven o'clock, and I feel a little cold. The rollcall was suspended, and we reorganised our tents. I was rather attached to our stone wall around the tent, on which we had been working hard for the past three months. Then the eight people whom I mentioned before settled into our new tent. (These people knew each other very well.)

In the afternoon people practised baseball or *sumō*. Grapes were received by the canteen. I was given a lot of grapes by Mr Sakimura.

20 March 1942

A clear sky. It was warm. Mr Hoshikawa and Mr Asano from the wood cutting group visited us.

---

18 *Shōgi* is a Japanese game similar to chess.

At two o'clock in the afternoon, I helped the new arrivals from New Caledonia to complete camp entrance procedures.

Goods deposited were returned to those who were detained in central Java.

21 March 1942
A clear sky. It was warm. I had a haircut. A third amateur entertainment show was held. It began at seven o'clock in the evening. People performed enthusiastically for two and a half hours.

22 March 1942
It was warm. From evening a strong southerly wind began to blow, and the weather deteriorated. Daylight saving has begun. We had breakfast at sunrise. At ten o'clock a *sumō* tournament started. General manager Mr Ozawa gave an address. Mr Yasufuku acted as referee, while Mr Hirose and Mr Tanaka acted as ring attendants. The tournament finished at half past four in the afternoon. Group A from Borneo won with a score of twenty points.

Mr Hoshikawa and Mr Asano returned to the wood cutting group.

23 March 1942
A clear sky. The weather was so fine it reminded me of autumn in mainland Japan. We played mah-jong with the group from Batavia.

24 March 1942
I was on meal preparation duty. I woke at five. It was still dark at half past six in the morning. At a quarter to ten we observed a minute of silence for the spirit of a person from the Ryūkyū islands who died yesterday.

Complete sets of clothes were distributed. We changed the straw in our mattresses. Today a Malaysian language course started.

25 March 1942
In the afternoon I helped to distribute goods. For lunch we had curry and

rice which we had not eaten for a long time. It may be a month since I last ate it.

26 March 1942

Fine. In the evening, a strong north wind began blowing, and it became hot and humid. A whirlwind blew over our tent, and it looked like the tent was covered by a smoke screen. The inspector came to our camp from the headquarters.

27 March 1942

Good weather. I went to the hospital to take a census of the camp population.

An intermediate Malaysian language course began. The number of participants was about one hundred and thirty.

Socks, T-shirts, long underpants, toothbrushes, and shaving brushes were distributed.

28 March 1942

Cloudy. A strong south wind blew. We were troubled by a cloud of dust. In the evening it started raining and the temperature dropped suddenly. For dinner we had *udon* [thick white noodles]. A preliminary round of *shōgi* was held. (The first and second rounds were completed.)

29 March 1942

Fine. When the temperature dropped in the morning, I even felt cold.

I was on toilet cleaning duty. The results of the *shōgi* tournament were as follows. The group from eastern Java gained fourteen points, the group from Borneo thirteen points, the group from western Java eight points, the group from Australia and New Caledonia seven points, and the person who won the individual tournament was Mr Yamamoto from Borneo.

At two o'clock in the afternoon fourteen people in the wood cutting group departed.

30 March 1942

In the morning it was calm and fine, but a strong south-westerly wind blew in the afternoon. The tent swayed badly. From now on we will not receive any newspapers.

At one o'clock in the afternoon an individual *sumō* tournament began. Mr Ishibashi from Borneo became our champion, and Mr Shumiya finished second.

31 March 1942

From half past one we had a consolation *sumō* tournament.

1 April 1942

A strong southerly wind blew, and it was cloudy all day. In the evening it became cold. At night I admired the beautiful moon. In the evening, an amateur play by *Akafuka-za* [the Red Coat Company] was held to welcome the new internees. The title of the play was 'A beggar and a payday'. It finished at nine o'clock.

2 April 1942

It was cold at dawn. It was a nice, fine day.

3 April 1942

A naming ceremony was held for our tent, as today was the Festival of Emperor Jimmu.[19] Today's ritual prayer offered to a Shintō god was as follows.

'With all due respect, provisional Shintō shrine chief priest Itonaga Nobuo requests permission to speak in front of all the gods and goddesses. We eight people were destined to live in a tent in the Loveday camp in Australia. As today, 3 April 1942, is the Festival of Emperor Jimmu, we eight people gathered here consulted each other, and decided to name our tent *Hakketsu aijitsu sō* [eight best people love day house].'

Of course, '*hakketsu*' [eight best people] referred to the eight of us living together in the tent.

---

19 This day commemorates the supposed date of Emperor Jimmu's death.

The number eight also referred to the following dates.

(a) The date of our arrest was 8 December.

(b) The date of our departure from the Sumowono detention camp was 8 January.

(c) The date to reorganise our tents was 18 March.

Next '*aijitsu*' [love day] referred to the name of the place where the camp was located: Loveday. It means that we enjoy each day. In the evening, the amateur theatrical company *Akafuku-za* [the Red-coat Company] went to the hospital to cheer up the patients.

4 April 1942

A clear sky. (It became cloudy later in the day.) An *igo*[20] training course began.

In the evening, an amateur entertainment show was held from seven to nine o'clock.

5 April 1942

A clear sky. It was warm. The rollcall was suspended, and our personal belongings were inspected. (Some people were frisked in the mess hall.) Playing mah-jong, *shōgi*, and *igo* in the tents became popular.

Some people complained about the distribution of goods.

6 April 1942

I was asked to oversee the distribution of goods by the army. I agreed.

In the evening I was given a tinned *kantō-ni* [a dish with various ingredients such as egg, daikon, potato, *chikuwa*, and *kon'nyaku* stewed in soy-flavoured dashi] by Mr Inoue, and I enjoyed it very much.

Two Taiwanese people of Chinese nationality departed for Java. However, on the way there they were repatriated back to Australia, as Java had fallen.

---

20 *Igo* is a board game involving the capture of territory using bead-like counters.

Birds in a cage, we console ourselves by watching birds.

Cartoon by Mr Ishikane.

7 April 1942

Cloudy after rain. It was unusually cold for this time of year. In the morning I helped distribute goods. In the afternoon I went to the office. I was on duty doing chores. I played mah-jong against the people from Batavia.

8 April 1942

Cloudy. I helped distribute goods.

9 April 1942

Fine and warm.

10 April 1942

Fine and warm.

11 April 1942

Cloudy with some showers.

12 April 1942

Comfort articles from the Red Cross were distributed.

The rollcall was suspended. Identification tags were formally issued.

The inspector came to the camp from headquarters. He inspected the mess hall while we were having lunch. It has been decided that butter will be replaced with artificial butter.

13 April 1942

Cloudy. A strong wind blew. The rollcall was suspended. I was given grapes.

14 April 1942

A clear sky.

15 April 1942

Fine. The wind was strong. It was cold at night. I was on dishwashing duty. Coupons for tobacco were distributed. I was busy distributing goods.

16 April 1942
A clear sky.

An airplane was flying over the camp all day today.

17 April 1942
Cloudy. It was cool.

18 April 1942
Cloudy.

A strong southerly wind blew and raised dust. We received a report from the camp commander about an inspection at the wood cutting camp. Mr Tsuda died.

The tents in the eleventh row were inspected. At six o'clock in the evening an amateur entertainment show began. We received a serve of sandwiches and a cup of tea. The show finished at nine o'clock in the evening.

19 April 1942
Cloudy with some showers. At half past three in the afternoon we observed a minute of silence for the spirit of Mr Tsuda.

20 April 1942
A Major General came from headquarters to inspect the tents.

It rained heavily in the evening. The tents leaked badly, and we were extremely busy fixing them. On top of that, a strong wind blew, and the tents swayed badly. I was present as an observer when the people from New Caledonia were given an injection.

21 April 1942
It has rained continuously since last night. Consequently, we did not have to water around the tent. From today we are suspending the morning exercises. We levelled some ground to prepare for a ceremony to mark

Tenchōsetsu [the Emperor's Birthday].[21] At six o'clock the canteen began selling cigarettes. We were able to buy ten cigarettes per person.

22 April 1942
It has become fine after all the rain.

An agreement has been concluded between Japan and England on exchanging internees. The first exchange ship will leave from Japan at the end of May and sail for East Africa.

The intermediate course in the Malaysian language has been concluded.

24 April 1942
We had great difficulty draining water around the tent. A preliminary round of trials was held to select runners for an inter-row relay to be held on 29 April.

In the evening it was suddenly decided to show us some movies. Movies such as one showing scenery around Darwin were shown.

25 April 1942
Fine. A light wind blew.

Straw was distributed for mattresses. This morning we had the first frost for the season. We changed razor blades. I was on duty setting the tables. (I got up at five.)

26 April 1942
Fine. We selected runners to participate in a centipede race [between teams of runners with their legs tied together] on the sports day to celebrate the Emperor's Birthday.

27 April 1942
Cloud clearing to fine weather.

---

21 A national holiday observed from 1868 to 1948.

28 April 1942

Preparation for the sports day. In the afternoon I assisted with the taking of fingerprints from the people from New Caledonia.

29 April 1942

A ceremony to mark *Tenchōsetsu* was held. We rose at five thirty and assembled at six forty-five.

First, we celebrated the long life of the Emperor and then paid gratitude to the Imperial soldiers and prayed for their continued good fortune in the war. We sang the national anthem *kimigayo* and a song to honour the Emperor. The compound leader gave an address. Finally, we shouted '*Banzai!*'[22] three times and the ceremony concluded.

At eight o'clock the sports day began. Fortunately, we had a fine day and twenty-five events were completed successfully. The results were as follows. The people from the eighth row won with the most points. The group from Batavia came second, and the group from Borneo came third. People from our tent participated in the centipede race and the relay and we came first in both events.

Today's meal was enjoyable. We had sweets and apples for breakfast, and apples for lunch. Moreover, tobacco was distributed. (We received twenty-nine ounces of tobacco per row.)

30 April 1942

Cloudy and warm. I was on duty setting the tables and I woke at around two o'clock in the morning.

Seven people in the wood cutting group departed. We had eggs for breakfast.

I assisted with the photographing and fingerprinting of people from New Caledonia.

Tonight, there was a beautiful full moon. In the light of the moon we listened to a story told by old people from New Caledonia.

---

22 '*Banzai!*' literally means 'Ten thousand years!' and may be translated as 'Long live the Emperor!'.

According to a report in today's *Advertiser*, 'Japan requested Britain to exchange eighteen hundred internees.'

1 May 1942

A clear sky. At around twenty-five past seven the sun rose in the eastern sky. I was lost in admiration as the sun gradually ascended.

The tents in the third row were inspected. In the evening we had an amateur play to celebrate the Emperor's Birthday.

I received a telegram [in English] from mainland Japan.

Japanese Red Cross request transmit Koike I.J. 50059.[23]

'Glad your excellent health, Fumiko.'

2 May 1942

A clear sky. Today's temperature reminded me of a spring day's temperature in mainland Japan. The office building is nearly completed.

The weather became unsettled. In the afternoon it began raining. As the night wore on, the rain increased. The lightning flashes were so bright that the clear shape of the tent was silhouetted in the darkness.

We were extremely busy preventing rainwater from pouring into the tent. We finally went to sleep at about three thirty in the morning.

Recently the grass around the tent has become green.

3 May 1942

Kerosene was distributed. The heavy rain from last night has stopped completely. After breakfast we fixed the drainage around our tent under a clear sky.

I replied to a letter from the Swiss Consul General Mr Morel,[24] dated 20 April, and requested they send a telegram to mainland Japan. The content of the telegram [written in English] was as follows:

'Am well. Don't worry. Koike.'

---

23 The letters 'IJ' here stand for 'Internee Japanese'.
24 Though he was Swiss, Georges Morel was not the Swiss Consul General but the delegate in Australia of the International Committee of the Red Cross.

4 May 1942

Fine. I spent all day in the tent, playing cards and *igo*.

5 May 1942

The Boys' Festival. For lunch we had *manjū* [a steamed bean paste bun]. A strong westerly wind blew, and a thick cloud of dust rose. Tobacco was distributed.

6 May 1942

I had a haircut. In the afternoon it rained a little. The wind was strong. In the afternoon I heard from Mr Andō of the Dōmei News Agency about the Tongzhou Incident.[25]

7 May 1942

About twenty of the internees are to be treated as prisoners of war and were ordered to move to the Hay Camp.[26]

Toothbrushes and flannel undershirts were distributed. I was on dishwashing duty.

At around noon, six planes that I took to be combat planes flew in a south-easterly direction.

In the evening we had a record concert.

8 May 1942

At around half past four in the afternoon we had a farewell ceremony for those who were being transferred to the Hay Camp.

In addition, thirty-one people from C Camp and eleven people from the Moorook wood cutting group are also going to be transferred. These people will be detained in the navy section of Hay Camp.

---

25 Also known as the Tungchow mutiny. Many Japanese civilians and troops were killed in an attack carried out by Chinese forces against a Japanese puppet state in eastern Beijing in July 1937.

26 From this time merchant seamen were classified as POWs rather than as civilian internees and were accordingly transferred to POW facilities, in this case at Hay in New South Wales.

At night, we had a farewell party organised by our leaders. Unlike the farewell party for the wood cutting group, it was a rather humble and sad one. It was cloudy all day today, and the sky was so dark it looked like it was going to snow. The number of the planes flying over has increased.

9 May 1942
A clear sky, and warm. In the morning we had a baseball game to farewell those leaving.

10 May 1942
Cloudy, with a strong southerly wind. There was a tent inspection. I sent a letter to my home in Japan.

11 May 1942
Fine and warm. I got up at six o'clock. I was on duty setting the tables. I removed small stones from the rice. After breakfast, those who were going to be transferred to the Hay Camp came to visit our tent to say good-bye. They were clearly sad to be leaving.

The Southern Cross in the sky was beautiful.

12 May 1942
The group of people who are being transferred to the Hay Camp departed at around half past four in the afternoon. No work outside the camp. We had showers and the wind was strong. Nine ounces of tobacco was distributed to each tent.

13 May 1942
Cloudy. It rained a bit. In the morning, blankets were distributed. In the afternoon, two hundred and thirty-nine new arrivals had a physical examination. The Swiss consul visited the camp. (At the time of rollcall, he looked around the tents. He also tried the camp food.)

14 May 1942
Fine. It was chilly in the morning.

The Japanese internees held concerts to entertain themselves and invited camp staff to watch their performance.

Cartoon by Mr Okamura.

15 May 1942

Fine after cloudy weather. I helped to conduct a medical examination. It was cold in the morning.

16 May 1942

After lunch I participated as a record keeper in the introduction of new group leaders to the leadership group and some others.

In the meeting we made a detailed proposal for the improvement of meals. It has been decided that once a week we will have no distribution of bread or meat.

9 May 1942

An amateur entertainment show was held from half past eight in the evening.

It was cold, as a cold southerly wind chilled our cheeks and our whole body. At night, the barbed wire was lit by the moonlight. I found the scene depressing. The sound of car engines breaking the silence is now rare.

10 May 1942

On 6 May the Corregidor Fortress[27] surrendered.

15 May 1942

A movie screening was held at nine o'clock in the evening.

Our three meals are generally as follows:

Breakfast: Oatmeal, Stew, Bread.

Lunch: Curry-rice, Soup, Sweet, Bread.

Dinner: Roast Mutton, Fried Potato, Bread, Rice, Vegetables.

17 May 1942

A clear sky. In the afternoon I assisted with health examinations. As sales at the canteen have decreased, we agreed to raise the price of tobacco by a

---

27 Also known as Fort Mills. Japanese victory here on 5–6 May 1942 confirmed Japanese control over the Philippines.

penny per ounce. In so doing we can extract money to pay for work done outside the camp.

While we had egg and cheese for breakfast, we had *gomoku-meshi* [boiled rice mixed with fish or meat and vegetables] and vegetables for dinner.

18 May 1942

A little cloudy. It was cold. I supervised people preparing meals.

The tents in the third row were inspected.

The following are the results of a baseball competition held between teams organised by districts. (The allied team means that people from Australia are combined with those from New Caledonia.)

18 May: Borneo versus Allied	12:1
Batavia versus Semarang	2:1
19 May: Surabaya versus Sumatra	9A:2
Batavia versus Allied	11:0
20 May: Surabaya versus Semarang	12:3
Borneo versus Sumatra	8:4
21 May: Semarang versus Batavia	11:8
22 May: Surabaya versus Borneo	11:2
Sumatra versus Allied	5:0
23 May: Batavia versus Borneo	7A:6
24 May: Sumatra versus Semarang	8:2
Surabaya versus Allied	20:6

(All games were won by the team listed first)

20 May 1942

I was on duty setting the tables. I got up at four o'clock.

21 May 1942

There was a rather strong southerly wind.

22 May 1942

Mr Inokichi Suzuki died. Recently the cosmos[28] has been in full bloom, and we had a good crop of snow peas. The spring onions are growing quickly.

23 May 1942

We observed a minute of silence for the spirit of Mr Suzuki. The tents in the second and third rows were inspected.

Now that it gets dark quickly, we need lighting for dinner. The sunrise was at seven o'clock. The weather has become like winter in mainland Japan.

24 and 25 May 1942

Fine. Stocktaking was done.

We heard that forty Javanese people who were on board the *Cremer* have been interned in C Camp.

26 May 1942

A newspaper reported that an internee exchange agreement between Japan and America and England would soon be concluded.

Recently making pipes and *geta* [wooden clogs] has become extremely popular in the camp.

Today I darned my socks using a needle. I realised how much I rely on my wife.

The moon was beautiful tonight.

We played a baseball game: Semarang versus Borneo. The former won the game with a score of 8:0.

27 May 1942

Cloudy. Today was Navy Day.[29] I was on duty setting the tables (from five o'clock). The commander was promoted to a Major.

---

28 The cosmos is a flowering plant in the sunflower family.
29 Navy Day was established to celebrate the anniversary of the Battle of Tsushima, in which Japanese naval forces delivered a crushing blow to the Russian navy during the Russo-Japanese War in 1905.

We had macaroni for dinner for the first time. We were busy making sandwiches for our amateur entertainment show. In the evening we had an amateur entertainment show to mark Navy Day. When the rollcall was carried out in the morning, goods which had been supplied were counted. Many soldiers thoroughly checked all the buildings, including the canteen and office, under the floor. They even checked the vegetable gardens, ditches, and toilets. As a result, hidden goods quickly piled up. Then they took away the confiscated goods by cart. It took the whole morning to complete this operation. Consequently, the baseball game was called off. At around half past four in the afternoon a person who was supposed to be the ringleader was interrogated by the commander. The hidden goods had been secretly taken from the army storehouse by some of those working outside the camp. Despite this incident, we asked to be allowed to continue working outside the camp.

28 May 1942
In the morning we put the confiscated goods in order. We observed a minute of silence for the spirit of Mr Eizō Yamashita. We had a baseball game: Batavia against Surabaya. The former won the game with a score of 12:6.

29 May 1942
A clear sky. The tents in the eighth row were inspected. The first mah-jong tournament was held. We also had a movie night.

30 May 1942
There was a strong westerly wind. It was cold.

31 May 1942
It was bitterly cold. The soldier who came to inspect our tents stole our tobacco, and he was punished for that. At rollcall, we have been answering 'Hai',[30] but we were told to answer 'Here, Sir' instead. We had *ohagi* [a rice cake covered with bean jam] for lunch, and satay for dinner. Full moon.

---

30 'Hai' is a Japanese affirmative response.

1 June 1942
Cloudy. It was cold.

2 June 1942
A clear sky. It was a little warmer.

3 June 1942
Cloudy. It was cold in the afternoon. There appeared to have been a frost. Two huts were completed.

4 June 1942
Fine. At night, the Southern Cross was shining overhead, and we had an excellent view of it.

5 June 1942
Fine. It was warm.

News: It was announced that from 31 May to 1 June, two Japanese two-man submarines attacked Sydney Harbour and one Australian boat was damaged.

8 June 1942
I was on duty doing chores. I had a haircut. Sunrise was around seven thirty-five.

9 June 1942
A telegram fee was returned, as it was impossible to send a wire to Japan.

Early in the morning on 8 June the bombardment of Sydney and Newcastle was carried out by two Japanese submarines, which later sank. Four bodies from the submarine crews were recovered. On 9 June, their bodies were cremated at half past eleven in the evening.

The American side announced an overwhelming victory in the Battle of Midway ... From fourteen to eighteen Japanese warships were damaged.

11 June 1942

Mr Imamura died. Those living in the first row moved into a hut.

12~14 June 1942 [sic]

We had a tennis match.

> 12 June: I was on duty setting the tables.

> 13 June: Treatment for roundworm was carried out.

14 June 1942

I sent a telegram to mainland Japan.

> We had no fresh meat today. We had no rice for lunch.

15 June 1942

I received a telegram [in English] from mainland Japan.

> 'Hope good health. Fumiko.'

> It looks like it is snowing.

> Many people oppose the order requiring them to answer 'Here, Sir' at rollcall.

16 June 1942

It looks like it is snowing. I helped to collect fingerprints. A baseball game was held between Rubber Mountain and Bank.[31] The former won with a score of 2:1.

18 June 1942

Mr Imagawa went to the neighbouring army hospital to be treated for roundworm. I talked to him over the fence.

18 and 19 June 1942

I supervised setting the tables.

---

31 The Rubber Mountain team comprised people who worked on rubber plantations, while the Bank comprised employees of the Yokohama Specie Bank.

20 June 1942

A sudden shower. We observed a minute of silence for the spirit of Mr
Hama.

We announced the winner of a literary competition which closed on
15 June.

21 June 1942

The wind was strong. We changed our blankets. For lunch we had cutlets.

22 June 1942

The current number of internees is 992. Amongst them those aged over
fifty are as follows:

The group from Darwin and New Caledonia	331
The group from the Dutch East Indies	90
People of Taiwanese nationality	32
Total	453

There are 274 people aged over sixty. (The oldest person was seventy-
five years old, and the youngest person was fifteen years old.)

A breakdown of internees

Group from Australia	49
Group from New Caledonia	393
Java Group from Galu	155
Java Group from Sumowono	167
Group from Sumatra, Jambi	13
Group from Sumatra, Pontianak	24
Group from north Borneo	64
People with Taiwanese nationality from Garo	12
People with Taiwanese nationality from Jambi	3
People with Taiwanese nationality from north Borneo	2
People with Taiwanese nationality from Sumowono	107
People with Korean nationality from Garo	1

Person with Korean nationality from Sumowono   1

Person with Chinese nationality   1

Total   992

A breakdown of people from mainland Japan by prefecture

Prefecture	From Dutch East Indies	Others excepting New Caledonia	Total
Kumamoto	14	140	154
Okinawa	32	89	121
Fukuoka	15	51	66
Wakayama	17	40	57
Nagasaki	39	1	40
Fukushima			39
Hiroshima			37
Okayama			33
Kagoshima			32
Tokyo			31
Shizuoka			19
Kanagawa			16
Yamagata			13
Yamaguchi			12
Shiga			11
Hyōgo			10
Toyama			10
Gifu			10
Gunma			9
Ishikawa			9
Chiba			8
Nīgata			8
Osaka			8

23 June 1942
A clear sky. The fourth hut has been completed. Tents in the ninth row were inspected.

24 June 1942
A clear sky. Movie day.

25 June 1942
Cloudy.

26 June 1942
Straw was distributed. Mr Shōhei Miyazato died yesterday aged sixty.

27 June 1942
Fine. We had a visitor.

28 June 1942
Cloudy. I was on duty setting the tables.

29 June 1942
Cloudy, then it rained.

The *Asama-maru*, with American diplomats and four hundred and sixteen internees on board, left for Lorenço Marques via Hongkong and Saigon. It was reported that at the same time an Italian ship left from Shanghai.

Recently more and more people started making hats and socks using blankets supplied by the government. We were told that it was prohibited to cut up the blankets.

30 June 1942
The distribution of underwear.

1 July 1942
In the evening we had a heavy shower with thunder. Using proceeds from the canteen, we had some oranges at the table.

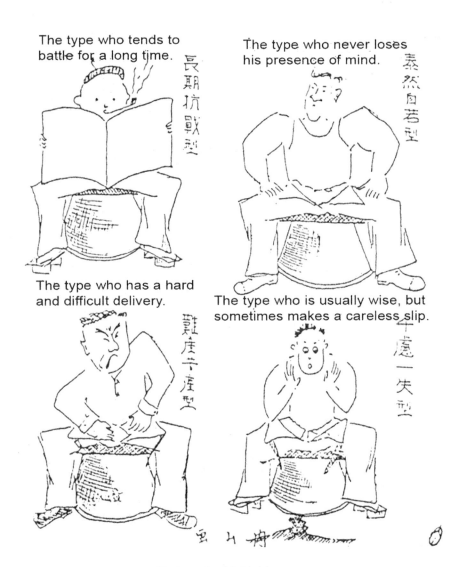

The type who tends to battle for a long time. 長期抗戰型

The type who never loses his presence of mind. 泰然自若型

The type who has a hard and difficult delivery. 艱難辛產型

The type who is usually wise, but sometimes makes a careless slip. 千慮一失型

Cartoon by Mr Uchiyama.

2 July 1942

The fifth hut has been completed. It has been decided that this hut will be used as a ward. Nineteen people were admitted to the ward. Among them thirteen people were transferred from C Camp and then admitted to the ward. Consequently, there are now one thousand and five people interned in B Camp.

At around half past eight in the evening Mr Takejirō Haraguchi was isolated.

In the evening we had a record concert. There was a baseball game: Bank against Mountain; the latter won the game with a score of 6:4.

3 July 1942

There was a strong northerly wind. In the evening, the wind intensified.

4 July 1942

Overcoats were distributed.

6 July 1942

Jumpers were distributed. In the evening we had a record concert. We changed razor blades.

7 July 1942

(I weighed fifty-nine kilos.)

8 July 1942

Fine.

9 July 1942

Mr Etsujirō Yamada, who was transferred from C Camp, died. He was seventy-seven years old. We observed a minute of silence for him.

10 July 1942

Using the proceeds from the canteen we bought sports goods and a gramophone. We distributed oranges for the second time.

11 July 1942

A record concert was held. From the proceeds of the canteen we presented five shillings each to one hundred people aged over sixty who were not able to work.

15 July 1942

Cloudy. According to a letter from Mr Kojima in the Tatura Camp, an exchange of internees will soon be carried out. Thirty relatives of the deceased went to clean the graveyard for the Bon festival.

The spirits of the deceased must be extremely glad.

Mr Miyamae was hospitalised. Straw was distributed. Judges came to visit the camp. (We requested clothes, food, newspapers etc.)

16 July 1942

Fine. We now have breakfast at a quarter past seven. The days are getting a little longer. We went for a walk in bright moonlight.

17 July 1942

Cloudy. We had a mah-jong tournament. In the afternoon, a strong northerly wind blew and it became chilly.

18 July 1942

I was on toilet cleaning duty. We had *udon*-noodles for dinner.

The results of the mah-jong tournament.

Team prizes: (1) Malang (2) Surabaya (3) Batavia

Individual prizes: (1) Mr Satō (2) Mr Ogawa (3) Mr Kadono

It has been announced that one hundred and five people from C Camp and six people from B Camp are to be transferred to the Hay Camp.

19 July 1942

Cloudy. Some people from the New Caledonia group moved into a hut.

20 July 1942

Fine. We had a farewell party for those who are being transferred to the Hay Camp.

21 July 1942

Fine. Those people being transferred to the Hay Camp departed at half past eight.

A newspaper was distributed. The eighth hut has been completed.

We were ordered by the Swiss consul to ascertain the number of people who have savings of less than five pounds and who are either unable to work or without a job.

News: One thousand eight hundred British people are to be released from the Far East as the result of an exchange.

22 July 1942

Fine. I was on duty setting the tables. I rose at five as I was on duty doing chores.

At five o'clock in the afternoon five people arrived from the Hay Camp. Four of them were immediately hospitalised.

(Although seven people were due to come to our camp, one person died in the Hay hospital, and another person was taken to the Melbourne hospital due to a traffic accident.)

25 July 1942

As the Axis powers did not guarantee safety of navigation, the Australian government delayed the departure of a group of Japanese diplomats and others who were waiting to be repatriated.

26 July 1942

For the first time a walk outside the camp was allowed, and one hundred people went for a walk.

A *shōgi* tournament was held. Mr Nakamura won the tournament. A second tennis court has been completed. At two o'clock in the afternoon the tennis court was officially opened.

27 July 1942

Fine. It was chilly. Mr Akio Mori was installed as a deputy compound leader.

Mr Shin Nakao from Okinawa died, aged fifty-nine.

28 July 1942

Fine. At half past two in the afternoon all internees were assembled. Then about two hundred and fifty of us were summoned and asked whether we wished to return home or not.

29 July 1942

Of those who were summoned, two hundred and forty people were officially informed that they could return home. Unfortunately, Mr Sasamura and I were the only two from the Yokohama Specie Bank who were not selected.[32]

1 August 1942

Cloudy. A shower. One hundred and fifty people went for a walk outside the camp. It grew cold in the afternoon. At around ten past three in the afternoon a solar eclipse was observed.

2 August 1942

A walk outside the camp was conducted today as well. Cloudy. It was cold.

3 August 1942

Those who are returning home were told that they will be informed of the time of departure within twenty-four hours.

4 August 1942

Mr Hikosaburō Shimabukuro died. Today I finished helping with the distribution of goods from the army.

7 August 1942

Cloudy. It was finally announced that the date of departure will be 11 August.

---

32 It is not clear why Koike was not among those selected for exchange, given that so many of his fellow employees of the Yokohama Specie Bank were chosen. The names of the internees were provided by the Japanese Government, but there was some confusion due to the romanisation of some Japanese names and the misspelling of Taiwanese names.

8 August 1942

The luggage being taken by the repatriation group was inspected. The departure scheduled for 11 August has been postponed. Today thirteen of those whose repatriation had been deferred were told that seven of them had been added to the repatriation group, and their names were announced. Mr Sasamura requested permission to send a wire to Tokyo to inquire about the matter, but his request was denied on the grounds that there were no mistakes by the Australian army in dealing with the matter. In the end, it was decided that the two of us from the Yokohama Specie Bank must remain in the camp. I spoke to Mr Imagawa (from the Yokohama Specie Bank), who was the compound leader of C Camp, over the hospital fence.

Due to the weather, an inter-camp baseball match was postponed.

A camp artwork exhibition was held. The works exhibited included sculptures, designs, portraits, trunks, *taishō-koto* [Japanese harp with two to five strings], guitars, *shamisen* [a three-stringed Japanese banjo], artificial flowers, birds made of buffalo horn, *kamidana* [a household Shinto altar], string bags, pipes, handbags, *go ishi* [go stones], *shōgi* [Japanese chess pieces], small boxes, mah-jong pieces, sandals, *zōri* [Japanese sandals], *geta* [wooden clogs] etc.

9 August 1942

A clear sky. Military currency was deposited for exchange.

10 August 1942

The camp artwork exhibition was closed.

11 August 1942

Exchanged currency was issued.

12 August 1942

Last night we had heavy rain with thunder and lightning. Today was the anniversary of my mother's death. I prayed that her soul might rest in peace. I was on duty setting the tables. Around noon it snowed. At around two o'clock in the afternoon some tents were blown down by the strong wind.

13 August 1942
Fine. A gramophone has arrived.

14 August 1942
At around four o'clock in the afternoon we were informed that the departure of the repatriation group is scheduled for tomorrow, and we had a small party as last supper for them.

15 August 1942
Those in the repatriation group started returning their three blankets and mattress at half past one in the afternoon. From half past nine in the morning a luggage inspection was carried out. I helped with the completion of no-claim agreements. At around half past two in the afternoon those leaving exchanged greetings with those of us who are remaining. Then, in alphabetical order, two hundred and fifty-nine people had a physical examination in D mess hall and were isolated in C mess hall. At around twenty past six, they passed by those of us remaining, as we stood in line waving good-bye, and went out through the gate. Then their figures gradually disappeared from our sight.

CHAPTER 6

LOVEDAY INTERNMENT CAMP DIARY. PART 2. FROM 16 AUGUST 1942 TO 15 AUGUST 1945

GENERAL CONDITIONS

On 27 July 1942, the names of two hundred and forty-one people were announced by the internment camp commander, and they were ordered to prepare for repatriation.

In addition, the repatriation of fourteen people whose names were unclear was held over for the time being. To my surprise, there was no mention of my name. The seven other residents of my tent were all summoned. I could not understand why I was not selected. Moreover, people related to companies were almost all selected in the repatriation group except for me and Mr Sasamura (the manager of the Semarang branch) from the Yokohama Specie Bank. The only hope remaining was that our names had been mistakenly communicated to other camps.

Gradually, the remaining names to be included in the repatriation group were decided one after another, by correcting wrong names or by assuming the names of companies that they worked for. As of 8 August 1942, the number in the repatriation group had grown to two hundred and sixty. Then some people declined being repatriated and others were added to the repatriation group. In the end, the number in the repatriation group was finalised as two hundred and fifty-nine.

Meanwhile, as I have already mentioned in the first half of my memoir, Mr Sasamura requested that a wire be sent to refer the matter to the Tokyo office, but his request was declined. Ultimately, we had no choice but to wait for a wire to be sent from the other camps. In the end, there was no news, and the fateful day of 15 August arrived.

(When the exchange ship arrived in Lorenço Marques,[1] our names were found on the exchange list, but by then there was nothing we could do about it.)

After that day I was forced to live a dreary life here in the camp for another three and a half years. On 29 July, Mr Okada succeeded Mr Sakimura as compound leader. In addition, Mr Masaji Nagano was appointed as the new office chief, and promising young men Mr Katsurō Chikanari and Mr Hideo Asano were appointed as assistants. Mr Tatsuzō Hirai became the person in charge of food related matters. I took off my hat to all those people who had sincerely looked after the repatriation group.

The only thing that those of us remaining could now do was to pray that a second exchange agreement would be concluded as soon as possible.

However, in the first repatriation group, several people were selected to fill the places of those whose repatriation had been held over. Some people from the remaining group began questioning the selection criteria for choosing the replacements. Rumours circulated, and many people began voicing their dissatisfaction. At the same time, although it was due to an error by the Red Cross, the fact that two of us from the Yokohama Specie Bank remained in the camp helped to reduce dissatisfaction in the group that remained.

It was also questionable that all the staff from Borneo & Co had not been selected. However, we could do nothing about it, as the war was a national crisis. There was no use in the remaining people complaining or being indignant over nothing. Compared to the hardship experienced

---

1   Lorenço Marques is now Maputo, the capital of Mozambique. In the Second World War it belonged to neutral Portugal. Exchanges of POWs and civilian internees took place via neutral ports.

by our soldiers on the frontline, or the hard work by the people at home backing up the armed forces, we did not feel any danger at all in the internment camp, unlike the detention camp in the Dutch East Indies. Consequently, I thought we should act prudently until the day when the next exchange eventuated.

Nevertheless, as the days passed by, everyone reacted to their situation differently, and some suffered nervous breakdowns. Because some people from our camp had already gone home, many of those who remained became mentally unstable, and began quarrelling over trifles. The most symbolic incident was the changing of the compound leader, which occurred like a 'coup d'état'. Those who were not happy with our leader's attitude towards the army authorities planned to replace the compound leader through the street leaders. First, they decided to choose the compound leader by voting, and then an election was held as planned. As a result of the election, Mr Miyamae, Mr Kuga and I were elected as candidates. Although I received the most votes, I feared that the whole situation might provoke the army authorities and that their attitude towards us would stiffen. I also thought that from now on the management of the street leaders' group would become difficult. Consequently, I firmly declined to become the compound leader. I requested that the street leaders' group should rethink and maintain the status quo. However, I could not persuade them, and Mr Miyamae, who came just behind me in the voting, was installed as compound leader.

Although Mr Miyamae played an active part, he incurred the displeasure of the army authorities. Then the position of compound leader was handed over to Mr Yamamoto from Borneo & Co.

The camp commander especially invited Mr Sasamura and me to the headquarters and requested that we cooperate with the newly elected compound leader, Mr Yamamoto.

Thus, the dramatic attempt to change the compound leader resulted in Mr Yamamoto taking up the position.

Mr Yamamoto took on Mr Sasamura as an adviser to strengthen his position, and he successfully performed his duty as compound leader until repatriation. Although the compound leader had to control the group, he had no authority. He merely liaised with the army authorities. Each group member made selfish demands and expected them to be met. It was the leaders' responsibility to persuade group members how unreasonable their demands were, and how difficult it would be to meet them. Because we were in abnormal circumstances as internees, it was hard for most of us to accept sensible solutions. I could not help sympathising with the difficulties faced by the leaders of the group.

Consequently, the leaders had to contrive various means to quell the dissatisfaction in the group. This involved encouraging sport, obtaining extra sports equipment, holding entertainment shows, record concerts, movie nights, and so on.

In addition, there were a few in the group who had specific skills. To utilise their skills, we bought materials from outside the camp and encouraged these skilled people to work on them. For example, some people made ornaments from water buffaloes' horns, and others made fishing nets. We encouraged people to engage in woodwork and tried to secure the materials they needed.

In the woodworking facility that we built, seeking the counsel of many people, many handicrafts were made using various hand-made tools.

On the recommendation of the camp commander, some of these handicrafts were sent to a prisoner of war artwork exhibition in Geneva ... (We did not hear any results from this until we were repatriated.)

It was also popular for people in the camp to make pipes, mah-jong pieces and *shōgi* pieces using eucalyptus wood.

Among the handicrafts were some marvellous mah-jong pieces, which were made from cow bones obtained from the kitchen. First, they made forms and polished them on the concrete floor. Then they drew pictures on the cow-bone pieces and pasted them to pieces of wood. *Shōgi* pieces were made from eucalyptus wood, and they were almost the same as real pieces.

These handicrafts were exhibited at the time of repatriation, and everyone marvelled at them.

Next, I shall talk about our cultural activities.

First, a language school was opened to teach Japanese to the second generation brought up in the Dutch East Indies. Various language classes were planned to prepare for the time when we would be released. From time to time, roundtable discussions on various topics were held.

In order to obtain pocket money for group members, we tried to secure work outside the camp ... (Some people criticised this, suggesting that work outside the camp would benefit the enemy, but we needed to have some work outside the camp.)

From now on, I shall briefly write my camp diary, relying on memos and on my recollections. In some places I had no choice but to suspend my diary. I did not include news about the military situation, as there were some discrepancies between the two [Japanese and Allies'] sides and much time had passed since the events. Daily table menus have also been omitted.

Finally, regarding communication between me and my family in mainland Japan, although communication by telegram was secured to a certain extent by the Japanese Red Cross and the Swiss consulate, almost all letters went missing, perhaps due to the sinking of ships.

I received only one post card written by Mr Chisui Koike from mainland Japan.

Although I tried to send a letter several times, only one letter was received safely by my family.

That's all.

16 August 1942

From today we will have no guard for work outside the camp.

18 August 1942

Mr Michitarō Hajō died. We observed a minute of silence for him at half past ten.

A tennis match (singles) was held.

19 August 1942

Four people in the wood felling group returned. At two o'clock in the afternoon, four people on the shift departed. Mr Huang (aged fifty-five) died yesterday. After a meeting in the evening between those interested and the compound leader, it was decided that a leaders' meeting would be called.

20 August 1942

Mr Miyamae's repatriation was cancelled due to illness and he was sent back to Australia. I exchanged views with Mr Futano, the principal of the Japanese language school, regarding Japanese language education. At around nine o'clock in the evening thirty-one people were arrested for gambling. (The following day they were released by the camp commander with only a warning.)

21 August 1942

We discussed commissioning lecturers for the opening of an English language course.

22 August 1942

Tennis matches between the huts began. In the afternoon soccer practice started as well. In the evening, an amateur entertainment show was held. The titles of the dramas were 'A dandy in Loveday' and 'The forty-seven loyal *rōnin* [masterless samurai] in Loveday'. The show was a great success ... It finished at half past nine.

The *Daily Mail* reported that one thousand five hundred civilians from America would be exchanged in Goa.

23 August 1942

A newspaper reported that on 20 August the *Asama maru*, with an American repatriation exchange group on board, arrived in Yokohama.

24 August 1942

In the evening I went to see how the students were studying in the Japanese language school. It was announced that the name of the exchange ship from America was the *Gripsholm*.

26 August 1942

It was reported that the exchange ship *Kamakura maru*, with British people from the Far East on board, had arrived in Singapore.

27 August 1942

Mr Lee Jin-cheng died. Today all tents were removed.

We went for a walk outside the camp. Using the proceeds from the canteen we presented four shillings each to the hospital patients as a monetary gift.

News: On 15 August, a major battle on the sea and in the sky unfolded in the Solomon Islands.

28 August 1942

We observed a minute of silence for the spirit of Mr Lee. It was decided that English, Chinese, and Malaysian language courses will commence on 31 August.

Mr Ōki fainted and died.

29 August 1942

We observed a minute of silence for the spirit of Mr Ōki.

Mahjong was a popular pastime among Japanese internees at Loveday.
Cartoon by Mr Ishikane.

30 August 1942

The first roundtable discussion was held for those interested. This was planned by me. I asked those people who played an active role in various places in the Dutch East Indies to come and talk. First, we listened to Mr Yamashita's talk about the island of Bali. However, unfortunately we could not find any material for the discussion. After that, we had roundtable discussions several times about other places. Unfortunately, we could not find any material. I had to reluctantly give up these discussions.

We had a visitor to the camp. The language courses began. Lecturers and lecture days are as follows:

Language	Lecturer	Lecture days	Number of participants
English	Mr Miyamae	Mon., Wed., Fri.	11
Malaysian	Mr Kuroshima	Every day	4
Chinese, Hokkien	Mr Ye Wen-yu	Tue., Thur., Sat.	25
Chinese, Peking	Mr Su Yen-ming	Tue., Thur., Sat.	7

4 September 1942

In order to relieve group ennui, lottery tickets went on sale for the first time.

5 September 1942

Sales of lottery tickets went well. Consequently, additional tickets were sold. The total number of lottery tickets sold was one thousand, at two pence per ticket. The results were as follows:

First prize: one pound each for two people.

Second prize: ten shillings each for two people.

Third prize: five shillings each for two people.

The remainder of the prize money was allocated to buy prizes for various events.

6 September 1942

A baseball game was held: all Java against the allied group of all Sumatra and Borneo. The former won the game with a score of 9:8.

7 September 1942

A second roundtable discussion was held.

A health examination was conducted for old people from New Caledonia. A rumour spread that this might be a preparation for exchange.

8 September 1942

Mr Sasamura became deputy compound leader.

11 September 1942

It was decided that from today roll call will be held in the huts.

We heard that the *City of Canterbury* with the repatriation group on board had arrived in Lorenço Marques.

13 September 1942

A judge, Mr Ray, visited the camp.[2]

14 September 1942

A third roundtable discussion was held.

16 September 1942

The baseball ground has been completed. The fence for the tennis court has also been completed.

17 September 1942

We presented gift money to the hospital patients.

---

2   The Australian military authorities appointed official visitors for internment camps in line with Regulation 9 (1) of the National Security (Internment Camps) Regulations with the aim that they would make regular visits to the camps, in large part with the welfare of the internees in mind. In South Australia the appointed visitors were W V Ray and K F Sanderson, both of them stipendiary magistrates.

19 September 1942

A baseball game was held: Java against Borneo. This was the third round, and the group from Borneo won the game.

20 September 1942

A walk outside the camp was conducted. It has been decided that on each occasion one hundred people will be allowed to walk through bushland to the bank of the Murray River. Thanks to the outing, we caught many fish with small bones, and they were put on our tables. A roundtable discussion was held. Soccer practice has commenced.

(Using proceeds from the canteen we bought various sports goods, and sports are gradually becoming popular.)

21 September 1942

I was on basin cleaning duty.

27 September 1942

Today daylight saving began. Clocks were set forward by one hour. From half past nine a walk outside the camp was conducted. I joined the walk for the first time. We walked through vineyards and pear orchards. I was moved by the pretty weeds by the road. Apricots had still not ripened, and I saw orange-coloured mandarins as well. As I had not seen the outside world for a long time, for a while I utterly forgot that I was an internee. Then we went to visit the graveyard for the Japanese people. We prayed that the souls of the deceased sleeping under the ground might rest in peace. Then we returned to the camp at half past eleven.

30 September 1942

Camp firefighting rules were announced.

On 11 September the content of the discussion with the Swiss Consul, Mr Morel,[3] was released, as follows:

---

3   Again, Morel was a delegate of the International Committee of the Red Cross; through him complaints from internees could be directed to camp or higher authorities.

(1) Regarding an exchange

In principle, an exchange agreement has been concluded, and most procedures have been completed. Unresolved matters were:

(a) the exchange place: Lorenço Marques or Goa.

(b) the exchange ship has not been decided.

That was the situation seven weeks ago, and these matters may have already been resolved ... Incidentally, the Japanese side has already offered to urgently send comfort articles such as textbooks, music instruments and food.

(2) Regarding the health examination of the old people from New Caledonia, the Swiss consulate does not know anything about (whether it is related to an exchange).

(3) It is not permitted to send telegrams to Japan. If it is an urgent matter, we can use air mail from Australia to Geneva, and a telegram will be sent from Geneva to Japan. The Japanese government must pay the fee for any telegraphic communication.

Requests from our side:

In general, the amount of any distribution is small. Please avoid distributing little by little, and distribute enough, so that everyone receives the distributed goods.

Spectacles: Please supply any spectacles, regardless of whether they are for long-sightedness or short-sightedness. If they cannot be supplied due to the high cost, payment may be made by the Japanese government.

False teeth: The same things apply as for spectacles. Enough should be supplied, so that everyone who wishes can have them.

Bread: Sometimes we have biscuits instead of bread. Please supply bread as much as possible. (Biscuits are not suitable for old people.)

Vegetables: We do not have enough green vegetables. Please supply those vegetables grown on the army farm by camp internees, rather than supplying them to private citizens.

Toilet paper: Although we had been receiving seventy-two rolls of toilet paper per week, the number of toilet paper rolls was cut to twenty-eight per week. We request an increase in the number.

Please provide more sports goods. (The rest is omitted.)

News: It was reported on 11 September from New York that Tokyo Radio reported an earthquake occurred in Tottori prefecture on 10 September in the evening.

4 October 1942
A roundtable discussion was held.

7 October 1942
Renovation of the recreation room began.

8 October 1942
Members of the amateur entertainment group began practising in earnest.

9 October 1942
Members of the amateur entertainment group collected donations for their services.

11 October 1942
An amateur entertainment show was held.

12 October 1942
An amateur entertainment show was held. The wood felling group was advertised.

14 October 1942
We discussed issues concerning the school.

16 October 1942
We collected donations for payment to the primary school teachers.

The amateur entertainment group visited the hospital to cheer up patients.

19–22 October 1942

A primary school play was presented at half past six in the evening. Everyone was impressed with their halting but enthusiastic Japanese conversation.

The rollcall was suspended, as training was held for newly recruited soldiers.

24 October 1942

The Swiss Consul visited the camp.

25 October 1942

A walk outside the camp was held.

27 October 1942

Soldiers moved by truck.

1 November 1942

Distribution of underwear.

3 November 1942

Meijisetsu [Emperor Meiji's Birthday].[4] A ceremony to worship from afar was held. At half past six in the morning we all enthusiastically sang the national anthem and a patriotic marching song. In the evening, an amateur drama night was held. Thanks to the passionate presentation by the amateur group members, the drama night was a great success. The titles of the dramas were *Akagi no komori-uta* [A lullaby in Akagi], *Shina no yoru* [A night in China], *Shūshoku shinsenjutsu* [A new strategy for getting a job]. And then *hanagasa ondo* [A dance with flower straw hats] was performed. Finally, we finished the night with *naniwa ondo* [A dance from the Naniwa region] (at half past ten in the evening).

4 November 1942

A party in appreciation of the amateur entertainment group (*Akafukuza*

---

4   A national holiday observed from 1927 to 1948.

[The Red Coat Company]) was held at eight o'clock in the evening. Eighty people gathered and the party was a great success.

5 November 1942
We were notified by the Swiss Consul, Mr Morel, of wires from mainland Japan. Mine was 'Family is fine. Hang on till the next exchange.'

8 November 1942
A walk outside the camp was conducted.

12 November 1942
We were told that within a few days a representative from the Red Cross will visit. We summarised our requests to the authorities.

14 November 1942
I was on duty cleaning basins.

15 November 1942
A walk outside the camp was conducted.

21 November 1942
An amateur entertainment show was held.

23 November 1942
We discussed food issues with those interested.

24 November 1942
The number of jobs outside the camp has declined.

28 November 1942
The new tennis court was completed.

29 November 1942
People are practising baseball and tennis more often, with enthusiasm.

2 December 1942
We had a visitor to the camp.

5 December 1942
Tennis matches were held.

6 December 1942
A baseball tournament was held between white team and red team.

7 December 1942
An exhibition of art by children in the primary school was held. The *Mail* newspaper reported that there are twenty detained diplomats in Britain. It therefore seems likely that a second exchange of internees will go ahead.

8 December 1942
Today was the first anniversary of the outbreak of war. We worshipped His Imperial Palace from afar and prayed for the Imperial Army's soldiers' continued good fortune in the war. We also prayed for the strenuous efforts of the people at home backing up the armed forces. Then we had a minute of silence for the spirits of soldiers who have died during the war and prayed from afar that their souls might rest in peace. I received a wire from mainland Japan: 'Our father is well. We received gifts (tobacco and chocolate) for our father through Mr Anazawa in repatriation group.'

Today's newspapers were filled with articles about the military situation, as it was the first anniversary of the outbreak of war. The Japanese side announced that casualties in our army from the commencement of the war to November were as follows:

War dead: twenty-one thousand six hundred and sixty
Wounded: forty-two thousand five hundred and twenty-seven
Battle planes lost: three hundred and ninety-four
Battleships lost: sixty-two (to 15 October).

On the other hand, the losses suffered by the enemy side were as follows:

War dead: fifty-one thousand

Prisoners of war: three hundred and three thousand

Planes shot down: seven hundred and thirty-one

Captured planes: two hundred and thirty-five

Planes destroyed on the ground: nine hundred and ninety-three

Ships sunk or damaged: one hundred and four.

In land battles on the Chinese front our army, with two hundred and fifty thousand soldiers, battled against an enemy with three million six hundred thousand soldiers ... On the enemy side two hundred and eighty thousand were dead and twenty-three thousand were captured.

On the other hand, the American Secretary of the Navy, Frank Knox, reported that Japan had lost many warships and was on the verge of a crisis. According to reliable American sources of information, while America lost less than one hundred warships, Japan lost four hundred warships, and so on.

Concerning the losses sustained at Pearl Harbor, they refrained from announcing the recommissioning date for the warships that were damaged, as it would benefit the enemy side.

Finally, when the war broke out, Japan possessed six million tonnes of merchant marine shipping. They had lost between one million and one million five hundred thousand tonnes to the present time ...

9 December 1942

A meeting was held about the school.

12 December 1942

A record concert and a public performance by *Akafukuza* [Red Coat Company] were held ... The titles of plays were: *Ninin baori* ['Helping hands' comedy[5]], *Yaji-kita dōchū sugoroku* [The misadventures of two

---

5 A performance in which one person wears a *haori* [a half-length Japanese coat] on his shoulders, while another person behind put his arms through the sleeves of the *haori* and feeds the person in front.

travellers on the Tōkaidō Road from Edo to Kyōto], and *Gekkyūbi* [Payday]. The concert finished at a quarter past ten in the evening.

13 December 1942

A party was held in appreciation of *Akafukuza*'s service.

15 December 1942

In the evening, the army band performed in their barracks. Recently it has become popular to grow watermelons, melons, and tomatoes on vacant land near the huts.

19 December 1942

A roundtable discussion was held.

22 December 1942

Mr Yoshihei Tsunami died.

23 December 1942

When the funeral was held for Mr Tsunami, we observed a minute of silence for him.

25 December 1942

A baseball game was held, white team against red team. White team won the game with a score of 8:5.

Today was Christmas Day. At three o'clock in the evening a cup of (low alcohol) beer was distributed to each person. As it was a long time since we had last had beer, everyone quickly became drunk.

26 December 1942

A baseball game was held. (This time blue team played against red team.) Blue team won the game.

27 December 1942

The final baseball game was held. Blue team played against white team. The game was a draw.

29 December 1942

A rematch of the final game was held. This time white team won the game with a score of 8A-5.

31 December 1942

It was still light at half past nine in the evening. Sunrise was at half past five in the morning.

1 January 1943

(New Year's Day) I got up at half past five in the morning. After having a bath, I waited for the first sunrise of the year. Soon the scarlet sun rose on the horizon. We refrained from New Year greetings, as we were internees. At a quarter to seven we worshipped His Imperial Palace from afar according to our established custom.

In a solemn atmosphere, we prayed for the long life of the Emperor and the prosperity of the royal family. Then we celebrated the prosperity of the Imperial country, expressed our gratitude to the Imperial soldiers, and prayed for their continued good fortune in the war. We observed a minute of silence for the spirits of those soldiers who were killed in battle to protect our country and prayed that their spirits might rest in peace. Then we prayed for the wounded soldiers in white gowns, for their wounds to heal quickly, and for them to return to the front as soon as possible. We also expressed our gratitude to those people at home backing up the armed forces. Finally, the compound leader made a New Year speech. We once again realised the significance of the situation and vowed afresh that we would do our best until the day of release. We had *ozōni* [a New Year's dish: soup containing rice cakes and vegetables] for breakfast, which we had not had for a long time. For lunch we had cakes and fruit which decorated the table.

From eight o'clock on, indoor games were held, and we enjoyed playing them enormously.

2 January 1943

In the morning, a north-easterly wind blew. It was hot and humid. In the afternoon, the wind shifted to the south, and a cloud of sand blanketed the camp. It was so thick that we could not see the huts on the opposite side.

4 January 1943

Two hundred people applied for wood felling work. One hundred and five people will be chosen from them tomorrow.

5 January 1943

One hundred and ten people were chosen for the wood felling work.

A party was held to recognise the service of the sports game staff.

6 January 1943

We had a visitor to the camp.

7 January 1943

Italian internees escaped.

10 January 1943

We had a rather cool day, for the first time in a long time. I was on toilet cleaning duty. A baseball game was held. Recently the days are becoming shorter, but it is still light until nine o'clock in the evening.

11 January 1943

A baseball game was held between young people from the second generation.

14 January 1943

A New Year's greeting from the Japanese foreign minister was communicated.

'Sincerest greetings with best wishes which joins the thought of your people at this New Year's season.' [The original was written in English.]

In reply, the compound leader wired to the Japanese foreign minister:

'Thanks [sic] your kind New Year's Message. Our people keeping well. 14B Compound Leader, Okada.' [The original was written in English.]

15 January 1943
I signed a medical check-up card.

16 January 1943
I received a wire from my wife saying that everyone in the family was fine.

17 January 1943
A baseball game was held: a group of language school students against a group from the public. The latter won the game.

18 January 1943
Medical check-ups began.

19 January 1943
It is getting a little chilly.

20 January 1943
Our group had their medical check-ups.

21 January 1943
I sent a letter to mainland Japan.

22 January 1943
We had peaches on the table. It was a rare occasion.

23 January 1943
The Swiss Consul, Mr Morel, visited the camp. The content of the meeting was as follows:

Issues regarding the exchange of internees:

An exchange is being negotiated between the two countries (Japan and Britain). The negotiations are deadlocked, as they could not find a suitable ship to transport the internees. The Red Cross was planning to use a

Renmark, May, 1943. Japanese internees leave the train that brought them from Hay on their way to the Loveday Internment Camp Group, Barmera.
(AWM 123032)

Loveday camp 14 B for Japanese internees. January 1943.
(ICRC Audiovisual Archive V-P-HIST-03289-07A)

Loveday camp, Moorook work detachment in September 1943.
(ICRC Audiovisual Archive, V-P-HIST-01883-15)

Japanese internees with wood carvings at Loveday, September 1943.
(ICRC Audiovisual Archive V-P-HIST-01878-13)

Japanese internees having lunch at their camp at Woolenook Bend, upstream from Renmark. (Courtesy SLSA)

Japanese internees splitting wood for posts near their camp at Woolenook Bend, upstream from Renmark. (Courtesy SLSA)

A work party of Japanese internees working on the river bank amongst logs near
their camp at Woolenook Bend, upstream from Renmark.
(Courtesy SLSA)

Loveday camp, Woolenook Detachment. (No date.)
(ICRC Audiovisual Archive, V-P-HIST-E-00319)

Loveday, March, 1943. Japanese internees use a cross cut saw to cut firewood.
(AWM 064826)

Loveday, March, 1943. Japanese internees placing offerings for the spirit
of the dead on the grave of IJ51875 Matsujiro Nakayama.
(AWM 064812)

Woolenook, 3 February 1944. Japanese internees leave their compound at 1645 hours, after dinner at 1600 hours, to fish and swim in the Murray River until sundown. (AWM 122980)

Woolenook, March, 1944. A Japanese internee sharpens a saw blade at the mill, Loveday Group, Barmera.

(AWM 122974)

Loveday civil internment camp 14 C. Red Cross delegate Dr Morel visiting a
shrine with Japanese camp leaders, July 1944.
(ICRC Audiovisual Archive V-P-HIST-01877-25A)

Loveday Camp 14C. Japanese camp leaders with Dr Morel, July 1944.
(ICRC Audiovisual Archive V-P-HIST-01877-23A)

Loveday Camp 14C. Group portrait of Japanese internees, July 1944.
(ICRC Audiovisual Archive, V-P-HIST-E-01085)

Loveday Camp 14C. Group portrait of Japanese internees, July 1944.
(ICRC Audiovisual Archive, V-P-HIST-E-01086)

No. 9 Camp nursery, Loveday, April 1944. Two Japanese internees on a 'Holland' celery planter being towed by tractor. They are planting guayule seedlings they had raised for trials to investigate the plant's use as an alternative source of natural rubber. (AWM 123079)

Loveday camp 14 B. Japanese wood-carver. July 1944.
(ICRC Audiovisual Archive V-P-HIST-01878-30A)

Barmera, 1945. View from the Southern Tower, looking north, at No 14 Camp Loveday. C Compound is to the left and B Compound to the right.

(AWM 122991)

Loveday, March, 1945. Japanese internees cut up tomatoes for seed extraction at No. 14 Gardens. Before the war the US supplied almost all of Australia's vegetable seed requirements but their export ceased after Pearl Harbor. To meet the threat of a shortage a large area was set aside at Loveday for a farm. (AWM 122940)

The band rotunda at 14C Compound at No 14 Camp Loveday, 1945. Each day some Japanese internees would play bamboo pipes and stringed instruments. The hanging object consists of varying lengths of bamboo and glass which produced pleasant tinkling sounds in the wind.

(AWM 122995)

A tennis clubhouse built by internees in 14B Compound Loveday.
(AWM 123014)

A landscaped Japanese type-garden built by internees in 14B Compound, Loveday.
(AWM 123010)

A Japanese shrine constructed by internees of 14B Compound, Loveday.
(AWM 123011)

chartered ship to transport them via Singapore to Japan. However, for the time being, they had no choice but to transfer via Lorenço Marques.

The number of internees exchanged was one thousand in the previous case.

It appeared that of late the Japanese government wished to exchange internees. However, the two countries appeared not to agree on the people subject to exchange.

The transfer of money from Japan:

The first amount transferred was £1,921, of which £1,000 was distributed to the Tatura Camp for the family group,[6] the remainder being distributed to B & C Camps.

As, unexpectedly, many people wished to borrow money, we requested that they send us a further £2,000.

Sending goods from Japan:

Although the Japanese government offered to send the required goods, it was too complicated to manage, due to the coupon system, which created special circumstances here. As it would be more convenient for us to distribute in cash, we are planning to negotiate with the Japanese government to send money.

Requests from our side:

As we heard that in the Tatura Camp £2 and serge trousers were distributed to each person, we requested that the facts be checked.

Issues concerning food.

Sugar: We cannot expect more than one pound per week.

Fish: As fish are expensive, we cannot expect any distribution of fish.

However, the Swiss are willing to negotiate about fishing.

Regarding the money that was confiscated in the Dutch East Indies, the Swiss would like to negotiate to have it returned to us. Regarding false teeth and spectacles, they would like to negotiate with

---

6 Japanese families, including women and children, were held at the Tatura Camp in Victoria.

the authorities so that we can receive them, even without payment.

The current number of internees is 742 persons.

24 January 1943

Inspection under the floor. An amateur entertainment show was held.

25 January 1943

Regarding the request for a money transfer from Japan, we came to the conclusion that we should refrain from doing this in light of the current situation.

27 January 1943

Although we asked Mr Morel to request a transfer of £2,000 from Japan, we formally cancelled this request.

29 January 1943

For the past couple of days, a strong northerly wind has been blowing, and it has been hot and humid. Inside the hut we felt as if we were in a sauna. I could not find anywhere to lie down, even though my body is small.

Among those of Taiwanese nationality, some lay down even on the toilet or bathroom floors to avoid the heat.

30 January 1943

One year has passed since we entered this camp. Today it was a little cooler. We had a feast of watermelons that we grew in the camp.

The repair of the gramophone was completed. Recently more and more people have started playing handmade guitars or violins, and the sound of music relaxes us.

31 January 1943

The last day of *Akafuku-za*'s series of performances ... The performance began at eight o'clock in the evening. The program was: *Koi no hatsutabi* [The first trip of love], *Yajikita dōchū sugoroku* [The misadventures of two travellers on the Tōkaidō Road from Edo to Kyōto]. The performance concluded at eleven o'clock at night.

1 February 1943

As it was hot and humid during the night, it was difficult to sleep. When I sought cool air outside the tent, I noticed the Southern Cross shining overhead. It reminded me of night-time in Java, and I became melancholy. Recently more and more people have begun feeding pigeons or budgerigars.

2 February 1943

As we had a southerly wind, which we had not have for a long time, it was rather cool. However, we were annoyed by gusts of wind all day today.

3 February 1943

I borrowed volume 12 of the *Jitsugyō no Nihon* [Business Japan][7] journal published in December 1933, and to pass the time I was absorbed in reading it all day.

4 February 1943

We enjoyed tomatoes grown in the camp vegetable garden.

6 February 1943

We began selling betting tickets for the baseball game to celebrate *Kenkokusai* [the National Foundation Festival].

7 February 1943

A baseball game was held: the group from Darwin and Borneo against the group from Sumowono. The former won the game with a score of 13–6.

11 February 1943

A clear sky. It was an ideal day for the *Kigensetsu* [Empire Day][8] ceremony to be held.

---

7 One of the first Japanese business magazines. The magazine was first issued in 1897.
8 Festival commemorating the accession of the first emperor [Emperor Jimmu] and the foundation of the empire.

A baseball game was held: the group from Sumowono against the group from Galu. The former won the game with a score of 17–14.

12 February 1943
Three people of Taiwanese nationality went to the hospital to give blood to Mr Ma, who has been admitted.

14 February 1943
A baseball game was held: the group from Galu against the Allied group. The latter won the game with a score of 9–6.

15 February 1943
Daylight-saving time ended. From now on the morning gathering will start at eight o'clock.

16 February 1943
Mr Ma died. He was buried at ten o'clock. He was aged sixty-four.

18 February 1943
As I received a letter dated 9 February, I requested a telegram to be sent as follows … 'Am well, Expecting earliest chance, Koike'. [The telegram was written in English.]

(The diary is suspended at this point, as I cannot find any memos except for news.)

18 June 1943
The occupations of the group from Darwin were checked yet again.

20 June 1943
Two staff members from the Swiss consulate came to the camp.
The content of our discussions was as follows:

(1) Regarding the exchange of internees: they had no precise knowledge. They had heard that a negotiation had been conducted with America. If a ship can be chartered, the British side will carry out an exchange.

(2) In regard to wiring mainland Japan: consult Mr Morel.

(3) Spectacles: ten pairs have already been distributed.

(4) Rations: we requested some fabric to repair clothes.

(5) False teeth: currently nine people are in dental treatment, and two people's treatment has been completed. We will report on the remaining people's treatment.

(6) Proceeds from the canteen are essential for us, as we have to use them to assist old people and to cheer up the patients. We requested them to negotiate with the army authorities.

(7) Food: we requested them to negotiate with the army authorities to increase the amount of white rice by 50 %, to replace biscuits with bread, and to increase the amount of meat, butter, and vegetables. We also requested an increase in the amount of seasoning.

An increase in work outside the camp would be difficult, due to a shortage of vehicles. They will consider the request for books.

In regard to twenty people who were transferred to the Hay Camp as prisoners of war (they used to engage in fishing in Darwin) on 12 May, this transfer was conducted following an agreement at a conference in Geneva. Perhaps a similar arrangement has been made in Japan. Payments for these people were: while skilled workers receive 15 pence a day (for eight hours work), inexperienced workers receive 7½ pence a day.

24 June 1943
We received a message [in English] from the House of Representatives by wire: 'House of Representatives passed a resolution on 27th Feb. '43, to express heartfelt sympathy with compatriot [sic] in hostile in relation severe countries and on behalf of whole nation, to send them warmest message of encouragement.'

1 July 1943
I was on duty setting up the tables. At ten o'clock in the morning

we observed a minute of silence for the spirit of Mr Okuda Yoshizō.

3 July 1943

Showers and strong winds. In the evening, an amateur drama concert was held. The program was *Mori no ishimatsu* [Ishimatsu of the forest] and *Tōchoku no yoru* [A night on duty].

4 July 1943

It was extremely cold. In the evening we had a second drama night.

5 July 1943

We had a visitor.

7 July 1943

We had a visitor.

8 July 1943

Fine. It was a little warmer. The hospital orderlies were on strike.

9 July 1943

I received a card from Mr Chisui Koike[9] (from Tokyo, dated 21 December 1942): 'We are relieved to hear that you are fine from Nihon Menka [Japan Cotton]. Everyone is fine except for grandfather. We pray for your safety.'

10 July 1943

We sent substitute staff from C Camp today, to work as hospital orderlies.

11 July 1943

Substitute staff were sent from the Italian Camp today, as hospital orderlies.

12 July 1943

Today we had a movie night.

---

9 Mr Chisui Koike was the author's nephew.

14 July 1943

According to a letter sent from the wood felling group, 'They heard from staff at the Swiss consulate that no internee exchange will be conducted this year.'

I was on duty setting up the tables.

(Entries suspended)

20 August 1943

I received a wire [in English] from mainland Japan: 'All Excellent, Keep Courage'

(Entries suspended)

1 January 1944

(New Year's Day) As I greeted the first day of Kōki[10] 2604, I felt tense. I left the hut early, at half past four in the morning, to do my duty setting up the tables. After washing my face, I bowed towards the motherland and waited for the morning gathering. By a quarter to seven all were gathered.

First, we worshipped His Imperial Palace from afar. Then we prayed for the Imperial soldiers' continued good fortune in the war, observed a minute of silence for the spirits of those soldiers who were killed in the war, and prayed that their souls might rest in peace. Finally, we solemnly sang the national anthem and shouted '*Banzai*' three times. Then the ceremony ended.

Today's menu:

For breakfast we had cheese and three rice cakes. For lunch we had fried fish and soup. For dinner we had one piece of rice cake. This was a special menu for New Year's Day. At around two o'clock in the afternoon a cup of beer was distributed. (Although it was called beer, it contained only a small amount of alcohol.)

---

10 The Japanese imperial year or 'national calendar year'. It is based on the legendary foundation of Japan by Emperor Jimmu in 660 BC. Kōki emphasises the long history of Japan and the Imperial dynasty.

Today was cloudy. In each tent everyone celebrated this pleasant day and a cheerful atmosphere was felt all over the camp, something we had not experienced for a long time. A group of drunken people merrily walked around to visit all the tents.

Unfortunately, a person in the neighbouring group became violent and it ended in bloodshed. We were too busy setting up the table to know the details of the affair, but I felt fortunate not to know the details.

2 January 1944
A baseball game was held (no result).

5 January 1944
In the evening, an amateur entertainment show (drama) was held with a lottery.

6 January 1944
For dinner we had small pieces of salmon.

7 January 1944
For lunch we had tinned salmon. It was hot and humid during the night.

11 January 1944
It was a pleasant day with no wind.

12 January 1944
Mr Tomiuka, who was on duty for chores, disappeared at midnight, and we made a fuss. Luckily, he was found in a different hut and the case was settled.

13 January 1944
In the afternoon we put wet towels on our heads to cope with the heat.

22 January 1944
It was hot and humid, and a gust of wind raised a cloud of dust. We sprinkled water on the floor.

27 January 1944

I wired mainland Japan ... 'I am very well. Don't worry. I am looking forward to seeing you. Please look after my father and child. Exchange appears to be taking a long time. Please say hello to everyone.'

31 January 1944

Recently the weather changes regularly. Hot and humid weather returns every two or three days.

(Entries suspended)

1 February 1944

I had watermelons and melons, which were grown in the vegetable garden inside the camp.

3 February 1944

It was reported that the American army has launched an assault on the Marshall Islands.

4 February 1944

I received a wire from the Yokohama Specie Bank.

'Your family all well. We hope you are in good health as well as high spirit. Striving for your return home at the earliest chance possible. Y.S.B.' [The original was written in English.]

5 February 1944

In the hut we all made a fuss about flies that stung us.

7 February 1944

A strong westerly wind blew. We could not see anything due to the thick dust, which reminded us of a Mongolian wind (yellow dust).

11 February 1944

From six-forty in the morning we had a ceremony for *Kigensetsu* [Empire Day] as is now our established custom.

Today's special menu:

Breakfast: Cheese, Cake, Canned beef.

Lunch: Sweet

Dinner: *Shiruko* [Sweet red bean soup with pieces of rice cake]

14 February 1944

I received a wire from the bank that enquired after my health and circumstances.

Consequently, I requested the Swiss Consul to send a reply on my behalf.

18 February 1944

Staff from the Swiss consulate came to the camp.

Regarding an exchange, nothing has yet been determined. We requested an increase in the amount of food. We particularly asked for good quality eggs and milk.

(Entries suspended)

8 March 1944

It has been fine for the past three days.

At half past three in the afternoon we observed a minute of silence for the spirit of Mr Yoshizaki Ichirō.

9 March 1944

In the afternoon, a sandstorm hit twice. We had heavy rain with thunder and lightning.

10 March 1944

We watch a talkie for the first time in a long time.

12 March 1944

The temperature suddenly dropped. Sunrise was around seven o'clock.

13 March 1944
Recently in the huts it is becoming more and more popular to play mah-jong and *hanafuda*.[11]

22 March 1944
I read a newspaper article reporting that through the mediation of the Catholic church, money transfers between Japan and Britain may be agreed to.

25 March 1944
A movie matinee was held in the afternoon. The movie was entitled 'Central Australia and the lifestyle of the Aboriginal people'.

A primitive way of life, in which life is in harmony with nature. A peaceful life in a remote area untouched by civilisation. The habits of kangaroos, emus, and antelopes [sic!], and the superstitious dream country where people eat green caterpillars. I was attracted to the life of naked cannibals [sic].

30 March 1944
It was still extremely hot.

1 April 1944
Hopes for an exchange are fading.

7 April 1944
Finally, we had some rain. I previewed the amateur drama presentation.

8 April 1944
From yesterday, works outside the camp were suspended because of the Easter holidays.

In the evening, a record concert was held.

---

11 A Japanese card game played with cards having twelve flower suits, one for each month.

9 April 1944

Works outside the camp resumed. I watched the amateur drama presentation.

18 April 1944

The weather has been unsettled due to the change of seasons. The watermelon and melon season has finished. I was treated to vegetables (such as daikon), which were grown in the camp, boiled and seasoned with sugar and soy sauce.

We observed a minute of silence for the spirit of Mr Morihito Majikina.

19 April 1944

The funeral for Mr Okano from Darwin was held.

28 April 1944

It was cloudy every day last week. We began preparing a feast for *Tenchōsetsu* [The Emperor's Birthday] tomorrow. We listened to records that we borrowed from C Camp (on 18, 19 and 24 April).

29 April 1944

It was a fine day, as if the day itself was celebrating the Emperor's Birthday.

We rose at half past five, and the ceremony began at six-forty.

We had cheese, soft Japanese sweets, and apples on the table for breakfast.

At eight o'clock we had a baseball game between the boys (no results). Then, we held athletic meets, refreshment booths, and treasure hunting, organised by the entertainment club. I sent letters to mainland Japan (to my wife and the Y. S. B.[12]).

30 April 1944

Athletic meets were held today as well. At one o'clock in the afternoon we had a movie matinee (on the scenery in Ireland, blood circulation, etc.).

---

12 Yokohama Specie Bank, his employer.

2 May 1944
The temperature dropped suddenly.

3 May 1944
It was rainy and cold.

4 May 1944
Cloudy and showers.

8 May 1944
A strong westerly wind blew, and we had heavy rain.

15 May 1944
A movie matinee and a record concert were held.

17 May 1944
Fine. We had our first frost.

18 May 1944
It was a little chilly.

28 May 1944
A drama was held.

29 May 1944
A movie day.

2 June 1944
A movie day.

4 June 1944
A *jūdō* room was opened.

7 June 1944
We received a wire from the Foreign Minister:
 'As I write this New Year card, I would like to convey my sincere

greetings for the New Year. Your health and welfare are always a great concern to me.'

We also received a wire from the president of the Red Cross.

'On behalf of six million five hundred thousand members, I wish each of you health and happiness for the New Year.'

14 June 1944
Vaccinations.

1 July 1944
I sent a wire [in English] to the Yokohama Specie Bank:

'Many thanks for your kindness to Family, Inform wife "Sincere congratulation father's 77th birthday". Hope all good health, Am well, don't worry.'

15 July 1944
Shrine for the hair of the deceased. A memorial service for the *Bon* festival.

21 July 1944
We had eggs on the table for the first time in a long time.

24 July 1944
The compound leader and street leaders resigned.

25 July 1944
A meeting of the group leaders was held. The candidates for the compound leader were elected by voting. Although I was elected as compound leader by the largest number of votes, I firmly declined.

(Several days later, Mr Miyamae became the new compound leader.)

12 August 1944
When a funeral was held for Mr Lee (of Korean nationality), I recited a sutra to farewell him. Although I was not confident in doing so, nobody wished to undertake this job.

In the evening, an amateur entertainment show was held in which people had to boast about their hometown.

News: On 5 August, a rebellion by Japanese prisoners of war in Australia occurred. (In the Cowra Prisoner of War and Internees Camp). 231 people died and 18 huts were burnt down. 108 people were wounded.[13]

We held a group memorial service for the victims.

2 September 1944

I attended Mr Hirahara's wake. I recited a sutra with those interested.

3 September 1944

A funeral was held for Mr Hirahara.

Fifty people attended the funeral. At a quarter to ten we began walking to the graveyard, which is located three kilometres from the camp. On the way there, I saw vineyards with fresh green leaves and pear orchards in full bloom. While I was fascinated by the beautiful scenery of the vast continent, suddenly a car stopped, and an old foreign gentleman got out of the car. The gentleman took off his hat and silently paid respect to the deceased. Humanity has no boundaries. I was greatly moved by this Australian gentleman's warm heart.

Since the previous visit, the graveyard is much improved, and it looks splendid now. About forty grave markers stood in an orderly line. About twenty Italian and German deceased are also buried there.

As usual the funeral began with words of condolence from the deputy compound leader. Then a representative of the attendees gave a memorial address. Finally, we recited a sutra. We came back to the camp at half past eleven in the morning.

---

13 The so-called 'Cowra breakout' from the Japanese compounds in the POW camp at Cowra in New South Wales occurred on 5 August 1944. Apart from the 231 Japanese dead, four Australian guards were killed in containing the breakout. In 1963 the Australian government converted a plot of land near the former camp site to serve as a war cemetery. Not only were the bodies of those killed during the Cowra breakout interred at the cemetery, but also those of the Japanese who had perished at Tatura and Loveday.

10 September 1944

At half past six in the evening, a ceremony for the fortieth anniversary of the enforcement of the Taiwanese Conscription Law began. Baseball games and a soccer tournament were held to celebrate the day.

17 September 1944

A movie day.

23 September 1944

We felt uneasy because our guards were being transferred.

Perhaps they have been sent to northern Australia, en route to New Guinea. Some soldiers were not happy about the transfer, and smashed windowpanes in the barracks.

3 October 1944

Fine and hot. From seven o'clock in the evening, an amateur entertainment show was held. The program was: 'a lottery, *fūingiri* [a love play ending with a double suicide], One night in the camp'.

4 October 1944

Planes frequently fly overhead.

5 October 1944

Mr Ōsaki suddenly died.

9 October 1944

I received a wire from the Yokohama Specie Bank.

'Your family members are all well. We pray for your health. We continue to do our best to achieve your earliest return home.'

18 October 1944

I was on duty doing chores. A baseball game was held for boys.

20 October 1944

We were troubled by sand and dust. Following Mr Miyamae's resignation,

Mr Yamamoto became the new compound leader.

22 October 1944
A movie day.

23 October 1944
I was on duty setting up the tables.

24 October 1944
We received a wire from the Japanese government, saying that we need not worry about support for our families.

'The Japanese government has taken all the necessary action with a view to affording assistance to the members of families in Japan of Japanese subjects interned or detained in enemy countries, that to say to the members of families who may be experiencing difficulties in the matter of their livelihood or education on account of the inability of Japanese subjected in question to remit funds to them.

The Japanese government, therefore, hopes that Japanese concerned will feel no anxiety in this regard.' [The original was written in English.]

3 November 1944
At six-forty in the morning a ceremony to celebrate *Meijisetsu* [Emperor Meiji's birthday] began. In the morning we had a foot race. In the evening, a children's play was held.

4 November 1944
In the evening, a group discussion was held about a novel entitled 'The Chastity of Husbands'.

5 November 1944
I was on duty setting up the tables. We were busy making pressed flowers.

8 November 1944
Last night we agreed at a meeting of street leaders to suspend work

outside the camp. This afternoon the army authorities informed us that if we suspended work outside the camp, they would close the canteen and stop supplying newspapers. In response, to stop the army authorities from tyrannising us, all members of the group determined to show the spirit of Japanese men, firstly by quitting smoking, and then by decisively suspending work outside the camp. Although the army authorities tried to set a moratorium for a week to consider the situation, we rejected this as well.

9 November 1944
Recently it is light from five-thirty in the morning till seven-thirty in the evening.

11 November 1944
A night-time roll call has begun.

24 November 1944
It turned out there was a miscommunication regarding work outside the camp. We came to a mutual agreement. We checked once again to see who wished to do such work. We will resume work outside the camp from tomorrow, 25 November.

25 & 26 November 1944
A play was held.

25 November 1944
I sent a wire to my family in mainland Japan.

3 December 1944
Yesterday Mr Ki Uehara died.
    In the evening Mr Toku Ōshiro fainted in the bathroom ... and died.

8 December 1944
The anniversary of our internment.
    The Deputy Prime Minister of New Zealand reported that an exchange

agreement between Japan and Britain would soon be concluded (in a newspaper article dated 4 December). Those British internees who wished to return home had already arrived in Australia on the *Wohine,* They were waiting for the exchange agreement to be concluded so that they could depart for the exchange location together with Japanese internees in Australia.

19 December 1944
A movie day.

25 December 1944
A baseball game was held.

29 December 1944
An amateur entertainment show was presented by representatives from each hut.

24 December 1944
An amateur entertainment show was held as an end-of-year party to help people forget the troubles of the past year.

25 December 1944
A 'baby golf course' [the original wording is in English] was completed.

29 April 1945
At six-forty a ceremony to celebrate *Tenchōsetsu* [the Emperor's Birthday] began.

From seven-forty-five on we had athletic meets and a treasure hunt. In the evening, a children's play was held.

14 August 1945
At dawn on 11 August, news about peace was heard over the fence from C Camp, but I did not pay any attention to it.

When the rollcall was made in the morning, the commander of the camp confided to the compound leader that he had heard radio news about the surrender of Japan.

15 August 1945
We were informed that a cease-fire had taken effect.

First, it was reported that Japan had surrendered unconditionally. Then the report was amended to say that Japan had 'Surrendered unconditionally except Emperor' [The original was written in English].

In the barracks, soldiers were in high spirits. However, as there was no work outside the camp, all of us shut ourselves in the huts ... It was a long, long day.

From today the information section suspended news reports. Then, it was decided that they would inform us of just a few simple items. Thus, attempting not to irritate the group members, they reported either that 'peace was concluded', or that 'a cease-fire was agreed upon', and they avoided the word 'defeat'.

However, as time went by, so-called '*kachigumi*' [that is, people who would not acknowledge that Japan had lost the war] emerged.

CHAPTER 7

REPATRIATION TO JAPAN
ON THE *KŌEI MARU*

PROLOGUE

On 15 August 1945 Japan accepted the terms of the Potsdam declaration, with the exception of the Emperor's clause, and a ceasefire was established.[1] From that time, we waited patiently for the day when we could set foot in our motherland. However, one day we read a newspaper article suggesting that the repatriation of Japanese officers and men from various places in the world might take ten years. We all became anxious, as we had no idea when our repatriation would take place.

A mood of resignation descended upon our camp. Once again, we had to consider how to spend our time in the camp. As it was difficult for us to contact our families in mainland Japan, we could not decide what was the best way to spend the coming days. In the end, we did nothing but kill time.

In these circumstances, some people became melancholy thinking of families left behind in their home countries. One day a person of

---

1   The original Potsdam Declaration of 26 July 1945 made no explicit mention of the Emperor. When Japan finally offered surrender on 10 August – after the dropping of the atomic bombs on Hiroshima and Nagasaki and the Soviet declaration of war on Japan – the Japanese government tried to maintain the Emperor's administrative prerogative but ultimately had to accept US Secretary of State James F. Byrnes's insistence that the authority of the Emperor would be subject to the Supreme Commander of the Allied Powers. When on 15 August the Emperor announced by radio his acceptance of the Potsdam Declaration, it was the first time most Japanese people had heard his voice.

Taiwanese nationality asked me to wire his wife to arrange a divorce. I told him, 'If your wife requested a divorce because you had disappeared and your location was unknown, it would be an exceptional case. On the other hand, if your wife bravely defended the home front, and was patiently waiting for you to return, it would be a tragedy to divorce her. Either way, you should be more prudent.'

On the other hand, some people set themselves a long-term goal. They began planting young fruit trees and were looking forward to having some fruit from them. There were also people who tried to make the wearisome camp life more enjoyable by having hobbies such as making *shōgi* pieces and pipes from eucalyptus wood. It also become popular to make *hanafuda* cards and mah-jong tiles.

Everyone, however, became pensive, due to the shock of the defeat. Some people became depressed when they contemplated life after repatriation.

Consequently, the mood in the camp become irritable. Even trivial misunderstandings caused tension.

As the days passed by, so called *kachigumi* emerged, who could not accept Japan's defeat and stubbornly believed in Japan's victory in the war. Particularly among the old people from New Caledonia, there were those who insisted that Japan had once again won the war, as she had won the Russo-Japanese War, despite the news announcing that Japan had lost the war.

When those of us in the information group announced news, we carefully avoided using the word 'defeat' and consistently used the word 'ceasefire'. In spite of this, we were called traitors to our country, and told that once we landed in Japan, we would be handed over to the Military Police, that we would be dealt with on the repatriation ship.

In fact, in C Camp the compound leader requested protection from the army authorities, so that he could avoid danger. In all the camps the compound leaders racked their brains to find a way to help people find mental stability.

Most people interned in the camp had been deprived of the foundation of their life, which they had worked unceasingly to build since Japan had declared war. Now they were worried about whether they could build their lives again, even if they could return to Japan. Even if they were fortunate enough to return to the place where they used to live, things would not go as smoothly as they had imagined in the camp. Consequently, they were depressed. More importantly, we had to work out the best way to spend time in the camp. The atmosphere in the camp worsened day by day.

The leaders of the group just worried about the situation, without finding any solution.

However, contrary to our expectations, it was suddenly announced that our repatriation day was set for February 1946, and, as the leaders of the group, we were relieved. As the repatriation day was fast approaching, I started putting my memos and diaries in order, which I had been writing since the day of my arrest. Among those in the first repatriation group, there were instances where all memos were confiscated. Therefore, in order to clear the inspection, I cut my writing sheets into four, wrote on them in small letters, and made thin paper rolls that I could squeeze into the corrugated carboard of a macaroni box. I hurriedly copied my memos every day.

In the end I managed to conceal all the memos in two empty boxes. Then I stuck some newspaper clippings to the bottom of the boxes. However, all my efforts were in vain. For this repatriation, we were allowed to take all memos and diaries, as the war had already ended. I was a little disappointed.

(Incidentally, all the memos that I brought back were numbered item by item. However, as I left them untouched for nearly thirty years, I found some bits were missing. I was disappointed, when I tried to publish them in book form, that I had to leave some gaps.)

Finally, the date of departure from the camp was set for 20 February. Before departure, the luggage was inspected and deposited with the army. Then it was taken to the repatriation ship by the army.

On that day, at eight o'clock in the morning, three of four of the distributed blankets were returned, but we were allowed to take one blanket with us. (God only knew that this one blanket would become our only protection against the cold.)

Then we climbed into a truck with a blanket and a bag containing dishes (this bag was made from a bath towel). We departed the camp where we had been accustomed to living for just over four years. I was reluctant to part from the people of Taiwanese nationality who used to study with me. We prayed for each other's safe voyage, and then we departed ... (Those of Taiwanese descent were mainly second-generation Javanese. There were about twenty of them.)

I told them the following:

'You will soon obtain Chinese nationality. Then you will join those nations who won the war. However, the communist army is expanding its power, and a civil war may occur in the near future. Please think carefully as to what you should do from now on.'

Among them, Mr Chen Xing-lai wished to come with me to mainland Japan, but he was not allowed on board with us due to his Chinese nationality. I had to leave him behind.

Incidentally, those of Chinese nationality were later repatriated directly to Taiwan on a destroyer.

(As a sequel to the events recorded in this diary, Mr Chen Xing-lai started a printing business in Taipei. He gradually expanded his business and began printing textbooks. He became the president of a top company and is active in the business world in Taiwan.)

REPATRIATION DIARY

20 February 1946

As soon as our group, which was divided up into several trucks, arrived at Barmera Station, we got on the train which was waiting for us. We set out for an unknown destination, leaving Loveday, to which we had become accustomed, behind. Although we were forced to live in the camp without freedom, it was fortunate that we were able to spend our time peacefully. Lost in happy and difficult memories, I farewelled the land to which I would never return.

The train took a straight course through the vast plain. From the train we could see vast undulating grazing land. I saw no herd of cattle or flock of sheep, but only eucalyptus trees here and there. Once again, I marvelled at the vast Australian continent.

Guards stood at the front and back entrances of the carriage to watch over us. As time went by, we became thirsty, but we had no way of obtaining drinking water. Finally, the train entered a train station, and sandwiches and coffee were brought into the carriage. We could satisfy our hunger and thirst.

When we finished eating, the train began moving eastwards again. When night fell, a lamp was lit by match, as there was no electric light in this old carriage. I was surprised to see the British way of life, in which people valued old things. The train advanced through the darkness, leaving behind the light that appeared to leak from the houses. Some people fell asleep, tired from travelling.

I could not fall asleep till dawn, as the train swayed a lot. As I was intently looking out the window of the train, I noticed people coming and going in a town. I realised that the train was heading for Melbourne. When the train stopped to change route, I noticed an old woman, sitting in a house located by the railway line, make a threatening gesture towards us with her fist. Perhaps her son was a victim of the war and she was showing her anger towards us. In any case, I realised that quite a few Australian people felt ill will towards the Japanese people.

21 February 1946

When the eastern sky was growing bright, I saw a range of high hills. Beside the railway line, fields of wheat spread in all directions, and the top of a mountain could be seen in the distance. For the first time in ages, I saw magnificent scenery quite different from the surroundings of the camp.

At half past six in the morning the train arrived at a station. For breakfast, sandwiches and tea were distributed. Near the station, grazing paddocks surrounded by wooded windbreaks could still be seen. Then I saw a flock of sheep grazing peacefully. Occasionally I saw a hare pop out, frightened by the sound of the train. Finally, the train arrived at the port of Melbourne. It was eleven o'clock.

Among the crowd beside the road, some people looked at us with scornful eyes. We felt deeply sorry for ourselves, as captives. Our group were taken off the train, lined up near the pier to which the *Kōei maru* was moored, and waited for the signal to board. The *Kōei maru* was a reddish-brown cargo ship which had been brought for the repatriation.

I was astonished at the shabby appearance of the repatriation ship, which I had dreamt of for so long. It used to be a splendid ship that carried silk to New York. I did not know what had happened to the smart passenger ships that I saw before the war. Once again, I felt sorry for myself, as a national of a defeated country.

However, even on a shabby ship like this, we would be able to set foot in our motherland. Cheered by this thought, we had a roll call and then walked up the gangway in alphabetical order with our luggage. I was filled with joy, as I was, indeed, free.

Inside the ship, the hold was divided into two levels. Although they were narrow, we had to endure them, as we were going back to the motherland. However, to my surprise, there was no bedding loaded on the repatriation ship which had come from our motherland. We just sat down on the floorboards. We had no choice but to settle down, placing the blanket we had brought from the camp on the floor.

Meanwhile, the first group of families from the Tatura Camp, and then the prisoners of war, came on board. Suddenly the ship became crowded. At the same time, various bits of news came with them.

The last group of prisoners of war came on board, and quietly descended to the bottom section of the hold. Every prisoner of war was dejected. The soldiers from the frontline were now captives. Perhaps it was against their will that they were returning home alive. I suddenly remembered the Cowra breakout, of which I had heard while I was interned. In Cowra the soldiers had rebelled in order to find a place to die. Sympathising with those soldiers, I felt sorry for the prisoners of war.

Later I heard that these prisoners of war attempted to riot on the ship. However, a navy commander who used to be the captain of a destroyer persuaded them not to revolt. Then all consented and returned to Japan ... We internees had almost no contact with them while we were on board.

It was awful that in this war, with its extended front line, those soldiers who remained overseas were ordered to kill themselves. However, considering how precious human life is, I would like to pay respect to the captain of the destroyer who ordered the soldiers not to kill themselves, and asked them to return home peacefully, so that they could help to rebuild their country.

At half past three in the afternoon, the *Kōei maru* sailed for Japan in the evening mist. Wafted by a pleasant breeze, we stood on the deck and watched the changing scenery for a long time, remembering various things that had happened during our long internment. Thus, we farewelled Australia, where we had many memories. In the ship, those without families were divided by gender, with family groups being accommodated in a different location.

The daily routine on the ship was as follows:

5:30 Rise, 6:00 Breakfast, 8:30 Medical examination, 11:00 Lunch, 16:00 Dinner, 19:30 ~ 21:00 Free, 21:00 Lights out.

Tonight's dinner was held at 21:00. We had rice and miso soup, which we had not had for a long time. We thoroughly enjoyed the flavour of our homeland.

After dinner, the transport commander (a former naval aviation lieutenant) briefly explained to the group leaders about the bombing of mainland Japan and then distributed a newspaper from that time. From this newspaper, I could get some idea of the situation in our defeated motherland.

When I returned to the group, I reported the news to the group members. Those who had stubbornly believed in a Japanese victory suddenly turned pale.

22 February 1946

The ship sailed straight for the motherland along the Australian coastline.

The sight of seagulls flying calmly was peaceful and picturesque.

We were broken up into groups of twenty, and each group elected a leader. The leader informed his group of matters that required attention. Medical consultations for patients also commenced.

23 February 1946

The luggage brought from the camp by the Australian army was handed down to each owner. Newspapers published in mainland Japan around the end of the war were circulated. (Of particular interest were reports of the bombing by the American army of middle-sized cities, starting with cities in the central part of Honshū.) For dinner, cabbages, salmon and tinned meat were distributed.

24 February 1946

In the morning, I happened to talk with Mr Nishikawa who was lost in meditation on the deck.

After graduating from Aichi Prefectural Middle School No.1, Mr Nishikawa became a fighter pilot, after three months' training. While he was battling in the skies over New Guinea, he had to make an emergency landing, due to an engine failure. While he was drifting on the sea, he was rescued by the Australian army, and was transported to Australia as a prisoner of war. The home he had left behind was in front of the Chikusa station, run by Japanese National Railways, in the city of Nagoya. Even if he were to be released after returning to Japan, he would feel reluctant to return home.

I told him that the attitude towards prisoners of war would be different from that in the past, and that he was now returning home by repatriation. I strongly encouraged him to return home without hesitation.

Furthermore, I told him that I would explain the situation to his parents if need be, and I would ask his parents to celebrate his safe return home.

(However, I did not meet Mr Nishikawa again, once we had returned to Japan. I do not know what happened to him after our return.)

25 February 1946
I lost appetite due to seasickness.

Today's meal. For lunch we had salmon, and for dinner we had a boiled mixture of rice and barley, and fish boiled and seasoned with sugar and soy sauce.

26 February 1946
The ship was becalmed due to an engine failure. For dinner we had *umeboshi* [plum pickles] and *rakkyō* [pickled shallots], which we had not had for a long time, and fish boiled and seasoned with sugar and soy sauce.

27 February 1946
The ship stopped twice due to engine failure.

At around ten o'clock I noticed that a destroyer, with Taiwanese people on board, had overtaken our ship, and then it quickly disappeared from sight.

As recently we have frequently been hit by squalls, more and more people are having a bath on the upper deck.

28 February 1946
Due to rain falling since last night, it was hot and humid inside the ship. Our meals are much the same every day.

The following is a story which I heard for the first time on the ship from a young officer (a second lieutenant) after we boarded.

'He had escaped into the mountains of New Guinea without food. He staved off his hunger by eating young tree buds, lizards, and insects. In the end, he was found by an Australian soldier, after he had resigned himself to dying from hunger. Then he was sent to a hospital in Australia by aeroplane as a prisoner of war.

As he was unable to stand, due to malnutrition, he had been crawling about in the bush. If he had fired his gun, he would have become a target for attack. So, he could not fire his gun, and had no choice but to hide from the enemy. He had experienced the misery of war with his own body, and strongly felt that we should never start a war. It was only natural that Japan, with its limited resources, was defeated ...'

1 March 1946
It was a perfect day today. We saw the vague outline of an island on the port side. The sea was calm.

In the morning we saw the Solomon Islands on our starboard side. Remembering the brave battle fought by our army, we prayed from the bottom of our hearts that the spirits of our fallen soldiers might rest in peace.

All the islands we could see were places where our Imperial Army had battled fiercely.

At noon we observed a moment of silence for those loyal and brave servicemen who had fought a daring sea battle off the shores of New Guinea and died at sea.

Our bodies drenched in the hot sunshine, contemplating the surface of the sea where the naval battle had been fought, we engaged in animated conversation about the heroic actions of our Imperial Army.

When our ship drew level with the coast of Bougainville Island, we were hit by a squall. We all went into the hold.

Although we discussed payment for tobacco and haircuts, no conclusion was reached. We could not agree how to pay after landing.

To begin familiarising us with the local situation, the bombing of the Gunma and Toyama prefectures was explained.

2 March 1946

A clear sky. Fourteen people applied to purchase tobacco.

A second local information session was held: in the morning, on Yamagata and Kyoto, and in the afternoon, on Hiroshima and Shimane.

We were approaching the equator. The sea was calm, but the mercury shot up rapidly and it became extremely hot. In the hold we felt as if we were in sauna. In addition, some people got sunburnt on the deck, and many suffered from it.

3 March 1946

At half past eight the ship crossed the equator. A line-crossing party was held, and we enjoyed an amateur entertainment show. In the evening, the transport commander gave us a talk. His talk was mainly on the destruction suffered in mainland Japan.

5 March 1946

The ship pitched and rolled badly. Early in the morning, when the ship traversed the sea off the coast of the Truk Islands, two fishermen's boats were found. We tried to rescue them, but they rejected our assistance.

6 March 1946

For lunch we had *kazunoko* [herring roe] for the first time in a long time. For dinner we had curry and rice.

At night, the ship started drifting, due to an engine failure.

7 March 1946

At around half past seven, the engine failure was fixed and the ship resumed sailing. For lunch we had boiled vegetables seasoned with sugar and soy sauce. For dinner we had salmon.

8 March 1946

For breakfast we had miso soup, which we last had some time ago. During the night, the ship pitched and rolled a lot.

9 March 1946

The ship pitched and rolled less. Today's lunch was curry and rice. For dinner we had soup with bamboo shoots. Today's temperature was lower than that on the previous day. I felt cold.

10–12 March 1946

Stormy weather. At night it became cold and it was hard to go to sleep. I spent the nights covered from head to foot by my blanket.

13 March 1946

At dawn the ship dropped anchor off the coast near Uraga.

Around nine o'clock it was announced that we would land today.

Around one o'clock in the afternoon the landing began. We walked to the camp on foot. On the way there, I noticed that many children looked dispirited. It was particularly noticeable that many women wore *monpe* [loose trousers with a drawstring around each ankle].

When we arrived at the camp, cherry blossoms were in full bloom. We were filled with joy at setting foot in the motherland. As soon as we entered the camp, we were drenched with DDT. Then we had a warm bath, which we had not had for such a long time, and we settled into our room.

After dinner, I parted with the people who had shared all my joys and sorrows for so long, as it had been decided that I was to be looked after at the Yokohama branch, guided by a messenger from the Yokohama Specie Bank. We vowed to each other that we would do our best and were unwilling to part.

Earlier, Mr Sasamura was welcomed by his family and went home a little before we did.

We heard that the prisoners of war were taken to another camp.

Those being repatriated to Okinawa were going to remain and live in this camp for some time.

It made a particularly strong impression on me when some men in their prime told me that they could not get a job in a fishery and would try to get a job in a coal mine.

14 March 1946
I left Yokohama early in the morning to attend a dinner party held at the main branch in Tokyo, which was organised by the president of the Yokohama Specie Bank. There I met my brother and my wife for the first time after such a long separation. When I heard that both had travelled with a simple packed lunch of rice balls, I became very aware of the shortage of food in mainland Japan. The dinner with the president, surrounded by other people repatriated from overseas, was enjoyable. We engaged in animated conversation on the hardships we had experienced in various places during the war.

After the dinner, we three returned to Yokohama. Then we departed from there by night train. We boarded the train at midnight. Unfortunately, we could not find any empty seats, and stood talking for a while. Then I heard from my wife that my father had died while I was interned (my mother had died from illness earlier, in 1927). Both my wife's parents and three of my uncles had also died. I also heard that my first son, who was due to be born in March 1942, had died a week after birth. Almost 11 years had passed since I left Japan in May 1935. I was, indeed, an unfilial son, who had returned home not knowing of my own father's death. The train was heading due west in the darkness. On the way, I was pleased to see Mt Fuji, as beautiful as ever, greeting me, a poor repatriated person.

15 March 1946
Early in the morning, when I got off the train at Nagoya Station, I finally felt that I had returned home.

Afterword

I have now concluded my description of the general conditions of my life in internment, which continued for more than four years. When I returned to mainland Japan, and saw that it had become burned-out ruins, I strongly felt the unimaginable misery of war. At the same time, I thought that I was rather lucky. Even though I was captured by the enemy, had no access to mail, and had to live surrounded by barbed wire, my food supply was more or less secure, I had no risk of being bombed, and was able to return home safely.

Next, I would like to pay my respects, and express my gratitude to the soldiers at the frontline, who fought hard on land, at sea, and in the air, for the Imperial country, risking their lives, and to those people at home who supported the armed forces, who survived air raids, overcame a life of austerity, and made a huge effort to rebuild our home country.

Finally, I would like to express my sincere gratitude to Mr Makoto Futamura, from the printing section of the Nagoya University Cooperative Association, for helping me to publish this book.

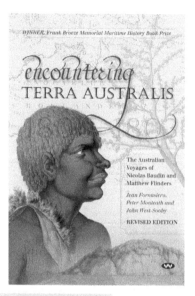

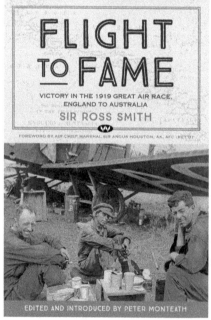

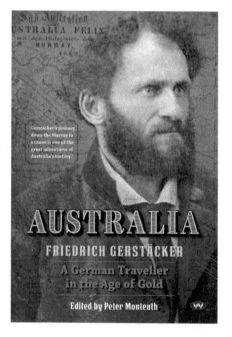

For more information visit www.wakefieldpress.com.au

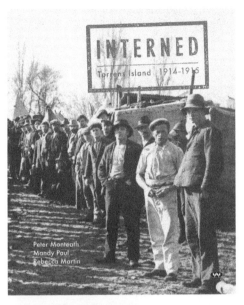

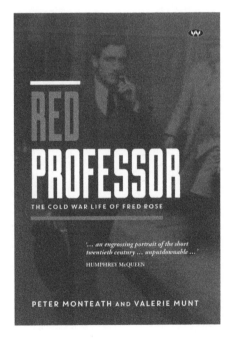

For more information visit www.wakefieldpress.com.au